53rd Edition

Travel to Cleveland Ohio

2023
People Who Know
Publishing
Jack Ross

Copyright © 2023 People Who Know Publishing

All rights reserved. No part of this publication may be reproduced, distributed, or transmitted in any form or by any means, including photocopying, recording, or other electronic or mechanical methods, without the prior written permission of the publisher, except in the case of brief quotations embodied in critical reviews and certain other noncommercial uses permitted by copyright law.

Printed in the United States of America

This travel guide is for informational purposes only and does not constitute legal, financial, or professional advice. While every effort has been made to ensure the accuracy of the information provided, the author and publisher make no representations or warranties of any kind, express or implied, about the completeness, accuracy, reliability, suitability, or availability of the information contained in this book. The reader assumes full responsibility for any actions taken based on the information provided in this book.

People Who Know Publishing

Forward: In this book, People Who Know Publishing will provide a travel guide of 101+ things to see, do and visit in Cleveland Ohio. We strive to make our guides as comprehensive and complete as possible. We publish travel guides on cities and countries all over the world. Feel free to check out our complete list of travel guides here:

People Who Know Publishing partners with local experts to produce travel guides on various locations. We differentiate ourselves from other travel books by focusing on areas not typically covered by others. Our guides include a detailed history of the location and its population. In addition to covering all of the "must see" areas of a location such as museums and local sights, we also provide up-to-date restaurant suggestions and local food traditions.

To make a request for a travel guide on a particular area or to join our email list to stay updated on travel tips from local experts sign up here:
https://mailchi.mp/c74b62620b1f/travel-books

Be sure to confirm restaurants, addresses, and phone numbers as those may have changed since the book was published.

About the Author:

Jack Ross is a college student who was born in Westchester County, NY. He's an expert on the local "in the know" tips of the area and is an authority on Westchester and its towns. He's been featured in several publications including Business Insider and CNBC for his books.

During his spare time, he writes, plays tennis and golf and enjoys all water sports (including his latest favorite, the eFoil). Jack also enjoys traveling and is a food connoisseur throughout Westchester. Jack travels consistently and has been to majority of the states in the U.S.

Sign up for our email list to get inside access to the towns and places we cover!
>> https://mailchi.mp/c74b62620b1f/travel-books
>> https://mailchi.mp/c74b62620b1f/travel-books

Table of Contents

Cleveland Ohio ....
Introduction i
History iii
Economy v
Transportation Systems vi
Neighborhoods vii
Food viii
Here are our ten favorite restaurant recommendations! ix
Nightlife xi
Local Traditions & Customs xii
What to buy? xiii
Finally, here are the five most famous people from the city! xiv
101+ things to do in the city xv
1. Visit the Rock and Roll Hall of Fame. xviii
2. Explore the Cleveland Museum of Art. xix
3. Take a stroll through the Cleveland Botanical Garden. xx
4. Attend a concert at the Blossom Music Center. xxii
5. Catch a Cleveland Indians baseball game. xxiii
6. Cheer on the Cleveland Cavaliers at a basketball game. xxv
7. Attend a Cleveland Browns football game. xxvi
8. Visit the Cleveland Metroparks Zoo. xxviii
9. Explore the Cleveland Museum of Natural History. xxix
10. Take a cruise on the Goodtime III. xxxi
11. Visit the Great Lakes Science Center. xxxii
12. Explore the Cleveland Cultural Gardens. xxxiv
13. Attend a performance at Playhouse Square. xxxv
14. Explore the Western Reserve Historical Society. xxxvii
15. Go for a hike in the Cuyahoga Valley National Park. xxxix
16. Visit the Cleveland Aquarium. xl

17. Explore the USS Cod Submarine Memorial. xlii
18. Discover the Lake View Cemetery. xliii
19. Attend the Cleveland International Film Festival. xlv
20. Take a ride on the Cuyahoga Valley Scenic Railroad. xlvi
21. Explore the West Side Market. xlviii
22. Attend a Cleveland Orchestra performance at Severance Hall. xlix
23. Visit the A Christmas Story House and Museum. li
24. Explore the Cleveland Grays Armory Museum. liii
25. Explore the Crawford Auto-Aviation Museum. liv
26. Go to the Great Lakes Brewing Company for a brewery tour. lvi
27. Attend the Cleveland International Piano Competition. lvii
28. Explore the Children's Museum of Cleveland. lix
29. Go fishing on Lake Erie. lx
30. Take a yoga class at the Cleveland Yoga Studio. lxii
31. Visit the International Women's Air and Space Museum. lxiii
32. Explore the Cleveland Police Museum. lxiv
33. Attend the Cleveland Asian Festival. lxvi
34. Take a tour of the James A. Garfield National Historic Site. lxviii
35. Explore the Dittrick Medical History Center. lxix
36. Attend the Cleveland Garlic Festival. lxx
37. Go birdwatching at the Lake Erie Nature & Science Center. lxxii
38. Visit the Maltz Museum of Jewish Heritage. lxxiii
39. Attend the Cleveland Comedy Festival. lxxv
40. Explore the Ukrainian Museum-Archives. lxxvii
41. Go ice skating at the Cleveland Foundation Skating Rink. lxxviii
42. Visit the NASA Glenn Research Center. lxxix
43. Explore the Dunham Tavern Museum. lxxxi
44. Attend the Cleveland National Air Show. lxxxii
45. Go kayaking on the Cuyahoga River. lxxxiv
46. Visit the Baseball Heritage Museum. lxxxv

47. Explore the Greater Cleveland Aquarium. lxxxvii
48. Attend a performance at the Beck Center for the Arts. lxxxviii
49. Take a ride on the Euclid Beach Park Grand Carousel. xc
50. Visit the Cleveland Police Historical Society and Museum.........................xci
51. Attend the Cleveland International Tattoo. xcii
52. Explore the Soldiers' and Sailors' Monument. xciv
53. Visit the Dittrick Medical History Center. xcvi
54. Attend the Feast of the Assumption in Little Italy. xcvii
55. Explore the Cleveland Skating Club. xcix
56. Take a tour of the Federal Reserve Bank of Cleveland. c
57. Attend the Tri-C JazzFest..cii
58. Go to a Cleveland Monsters hockey game...ciii
59. Visit the William G. Mather Museum. cv
60. Explore the Warther Museum and Gardens. cvi
61. Attend the Cleveland Pride Parade and Festival. cviii
62. Visit the Cleveland Hungarian Heritage Society. cix
63. Go to a Cleveland Gladiators arena football game..cxi
64. Explore the Ukrainian Museum-Archives..cxii
65. Attend the Cleveland Kurentovanje Festival. cxiii
66. Take a scenic drive along the Lake Erie Coastal Ohio Trail. cxv
67. Go horseback riding in the Metroparks..cxvii
68. Visit the Dittrick Medical History Center. cxviii
69. Attend the Cleveland Museum of Natural History's Think & Drink series.cxix
70. Explore the Italian Cultural Garden. cxx
71. Take a cooking class at the Loretta Paganini School of Cooking. cxxii
72. Visit the Cleveland Hungarian Heritage Museum. cxxiii
73. Attend the Cleveland Labor Day Oktoberfest. cxxv
74. Explore the Estonian Cultural Garden..cxxvi
75. Go ziplining at Common Ground Canopy Tours. cxxvii
76. Visit the American Police Motorcycle Museum. cxxix

77. Explore the Slavic Village neighborhood..cxxx

78. Attend the Serbian Cultural Garden's Serbian Festival. cxxxii

79. Take a scenic drive along the Covered Bridge Tour Route. cxxxiii

80. Visit the Greater Cleveland Aquarium's 230,000-gallon shark exhibit...cxxxiv

81. Attend the Cleveland One World Festival. cxxxvi

82. Explore the Slovenian Museum and Archives. cxxxvii

83. Go on a wine tour of Ohio's wine country..cxxxix

84. Visit the Playhouse Square chandelier. cxl

85. Attend the Great Lakes Burning River Fest. cxlii

86. Explore the Irish Cultural Garden. cxliii

87. Take a pottery or ceramics class at the Cleveland Institute of Art. cxlv

88. Attend the Cleveland Tall Ships Festival. cxlvi

89. Visit the Greater Cleveland Film Commission. cxlviii

90. Explore the Arabic Cultural Garden...cxlix

91. Go sailing on Lake Erie..cli

92. Attend the Cleveland Whiskey Festival. clii

93. Visit the Cleveland Firefighters Memorial...cliv

94. Explore the Shakespeare Garden...clv

95. Attend the Brite Winter Festival. clvi

96. Take a ride on the Lolly the Trolley tour. clviii

97. Visit the "Free Stamp" sculpture. clx

98. Attend the Cleveland Asian Lantern Festival. clxi

99. Explore the Ariel Pearl Center. clxiii

100. Go on a Cleveland Brewery Tour. clxiv

101. Visit the Nature Center at Shaker Lakes. clxv

102. Attend the Cleveland Dragon Boat Festival...clxvii

103. Explore the Rockefeller Park Greenhouse. clxix

104. Take a scenic drive along the Ohio & Erie Canal Towpath Trail. clxx

105. Visit the Cleveland Pops Orchestra..clxxii

106. Attend a performance at the Near West Theatre....................................clxxiii

107. Explore the Cultural Gardens at Wade Oval. clxxv
108. Go paddleboarding on the Cuyahoga River. clxxvii
109. Attend the Feast of St. Augustine in Tremont. clxxviii
110. Visit the Cleveland Pickle. clxxx
Conclusion clxxxii
References clxxxiv

Travel to Cleveland Ohio

Cleveland Ohio

State: Ohio
Population: 372,624
Ranking in U.S.: N/A
County: Cuyahoga
Founded: 1796
Tag line: N/A

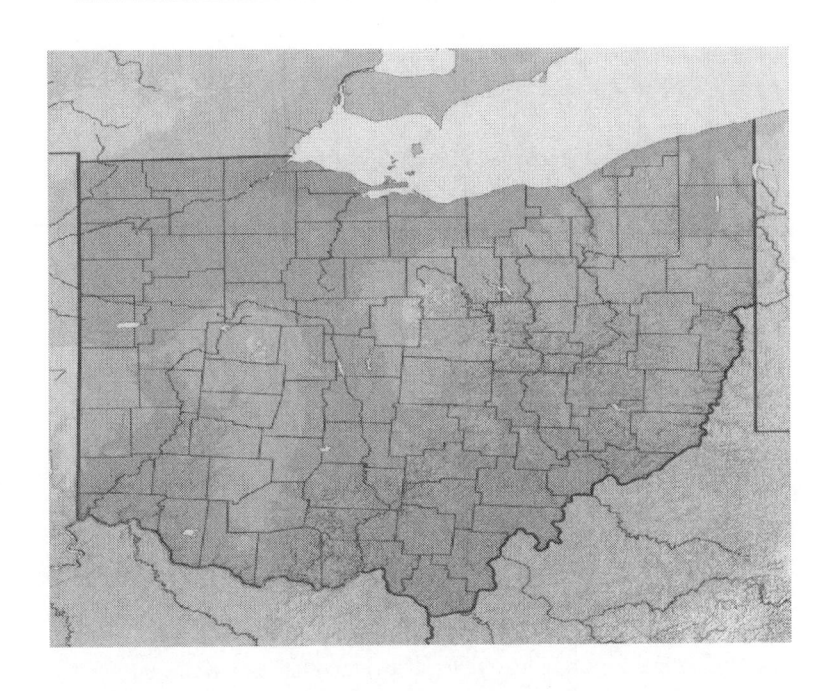

Introduction

Drew Carey: "I love Cleveland, and I think Cleveland is a great town."

Cleveland, often referred to as "The Forest City" or "The Rock 'n' Roll Capital of the World," is a vibrant and historically significant city located in the northeastern part of the state of Ohio, in the United States. Nestled along the southern shores of Lake Erie, Cleveland is a city with a rich cultural heritage, a diverse population, and a strong industrial history that has shaped its character.

Historical Significance: Founded in 1796, Cleveland has a deep historical legacy. It played a pivotal role in the industrialization of the United States and was a hub for manufacturing and steel production during the late 19th and early 20th centuries.

Cultural Hub: Cleveland is known for its vibrant cultural scene. It is home to world-class museums, including the Cleveland Museum of Art and the Rock and Roll Hall of Fame, which celebrate art and music. The city also boasts a thriving theater and performing arts community.

Sports Enthusiast's Paradise: Sports are a significant part of Cleveland's identity. The city is home to passionate sports fans who support teams like the Cleveland Browns (NFL), Cleveland Cavaliers (NBA), and Cleveland Guardians (MLB).

Lake Erie: Cleveland's location along the shores of Lake Erie provides opportunities for outdoor activities, including boating, fishing, and hiking in nearby parks.

Healthcare and Education: The city is renowned for its world-class healthcare institutions, including the Cleveland Clinic, one of the top-ranked hospitals in the United States. Cleveland is also home to prestigious universities and research centers.

Diverse Communities: Cleveland is known for its diverse population, which contributes to its cultural richness and culinary diversity. Various neighborhoods showcase unique characteristics and traditions.

Economic Revitalization: In recent years, Cleveland has experienced a revitalization of its downtown area, with new developments, businesses, and entertainment options contributing to its modern appeal.

Travel to Cleveland Ohio

Transportation Hub: The city's transportation infrastructure includes a major international airport, an extensive highway network, and public transportation services.

Cleveland's unique blend of history, culture, and a resilient spirit makes it a compelling destination for visitors and a dynamic place to live for its residents. Whether you're interested in exploring its museums, enjoying its culinary scene, or attending a sports game, Cleveland has something to offer everyone.

People Who Know Publishing

History

Travel to Cleveland Ohio

Initially, Cleveland was a small village with a few log cabins, and its growth was slow. The settlement's early economy relied on fur trading and agriculture.

In the early 19th century, the construction of the Ohio and Erie Canal (completed in 1832) and the arrival of the railroad (in the 1850s) spurred significant economic growth. Cleveland became a transportation hub, facilitating the movement of goods and people between the Great Lakes and the Ohio River.

Industrialization and Economic Expansion (Late 19th - Early 20th Century):

The late 19th and early 20th centuries marked a period of rapid industrialization for Cleveland. The city's proximity to Lake Erie and natural resources like iron ore and coal made it an ideal location for manufacturing and steel production.

Early Settlement and Growth (1790s-1830s):

Cleveland's history begins in 1796 when General Moses Cleaveland and a surveying party arrived to lay out the town. The settlement was named "Cleaveland" in honor of General Cleaveland but later had the "a" dropped from its name.

People Who Know Publishing

Travel to Cleveland Ohio

Cultural and Civic Achievements (Mid-20th Century):

Cleveland continued to grow in the mid-20th century, becoming one of the country's major industrial centers.
The city made significant contributions to the world of music, particularly in rock and roll. The Rock and Roll Hall of Fame and Museum was established in Cleveland in 1995, honoring the genre's pioneers.

Challenges and Revitalization (Late 20th Century - Present):

Like many Rust Belt cities, Cleveland faced economic challenges in the latter half of the 20th century as industries declined, leading to job losses and population decline. However, the city has undergone a revitalization effort in recent years. Downtown Cleveland has seen significant redevelopment, including the construction of sports stadiums, a casino, and a convention center.

Industries such as steel, oil, and manufacturing thrived. John D. Rockefeller's Standard Oil Company was founded in Cleveland. The city's population boomed as immigrants from Europe and African Americans from the South moved to Cleveland for job opportunities. Cultural institutions like the Cleveland Museum of Art and the Cleveland Orchestra were established during this time, reflecting the city's growing prosperity.

People Who Know Publishing

Travel to Cleveland Ohio

Economy

Cleveland, Ohio, has a diverse and evolving economy with strengths in various sectors. Here's an overview of its economy:

One of the major drivers of Cleveland's economy is the healthcare sector. The city is home to the renowned Cleveland Clinic, University Hospitals, and other leading medical institutions. These organizations provide world-class healthcare services and contribute significantly to the local economy. Biotechnology and medical research also play a vital role in the region.

Manufacturing has a historic presence in Cleveland's economy, dating back to its industrialization in the late 19th century. While the sector has evolved and diversified, manufacturing still plays a crucial role, particularly in the production of automotive components, aerospace equipment, and advanced materials.

Cleveland has been fostering a growing technology and innovation ecosystem. The city is home to technology startups, research institutions, and incubators, contributing to the development of new technologies and businesses.

The financial sector, including banking and insurance, is another significant component of Cleveland's economy. Key financial institutions have a presence in the city, providing a range of financial services to residents and businesses.

Cleveland is home to several universities and research institutions, such as Case Western Reserve University and Cleveland State University. These institutions contribute to research and development, innovation, and education, creating a knowledge-based economy.

A wide range of professional services, including law firms, consulting firms, and engineering companies, operate in Cleveland, serving businesses in the region.

The arts and culture sector also makes a substantial contribution to the city's economy. The Playhouse Square theater district, museums, and cultural events attract both residents and tourists, generating economic activity.

Professional sports teams, including the Cleveland Cavaliers (NBA) and Cleveland Guardians (MLB), contribute to the economy through ticket sales, merchandise, and tourism related to sporting events and entertainment.

Transportation Systems

Roads and Highways:
Cleveland is served by an extensive network of roads and highways, including major interstate highways such as I-90, I-71, and I-77. These highways connect the city to other major cities in the region, facilitating the movement of goods and people.

Public Transit:
The Greater Cleveland Regional Transit Authority (RTA) operates the public transit system in the city. This includes buses and the Cleveland Rapid Transit system, known as the "RTA Rapid Transit" or simply "The Rapid." The Rapid includes both light rail and heavy rail lines, providing convenient access to various neighborhoods and suburbs.

Airports:
Cleveland Hopkins International Airport is the primary airport serving the city. It offers domestic and limited international flights, making it a key gateway to the region. Additionally, Burke Lakefront Airport, a smaller general aviation airport, is located near downtown Cleveland.

Port of Cleveland:
Situated on the southern shore of Lake Erie, the Port of Cleveland is a major Great Lakes port. It handles a variety of cargo, including bulk commodities and containerized goods, and plays a vital role in regional trade and transportation.

Bicycling and Pedestrian Infrastructure:
Cleveland has been working to improve its bicycle and pedestrian infrastructure, including the development of bike lanes, pedestrian-friendly streetscapes, and dedicated trails. The city's efforts aim to promote alternative modes of transportation and enhance safety for cyclists and pedestrians.

Ridesharing and Taxis:
Ridesharing services like Uber and Lyft operate in Cleveland, providing convenient options for on-demand transportation. Traditional taxi services are also available throughout the city.

Car Rentals:
Various car rental agencies have a presence in Cleveland, offering rental vehicles for travelers and residents who need access to a car.

Travel to Cleveland Ohio

Neighborhoods

Downtown Cleveland: Downtown is the heart of the city, known for its revitalization efforts in recent years. It's home to attractions like Playhouse Square, Progressive Field (home of the Cleveland Guardians), Rocket Mortgage FieldHouse (home of the Cleveland Cavaliers), and a variety of restaurants, bars, and entertainment venues.

Ohio City: Located just west of downtown, Ohio City is known for its vibrant arts scene, historic architecture, and the popular West Side Market. It's a hotspot for craft breweries, trendy restaurants, and boutiques.

Tremont: Adjacent to Ohio City, Tremont features picturesque streets lined with historic homes, art galleries, and a lively dining scene. It's also known for its annual Arts and Cultural Festival.

University Circle: Home to several universities, museums, and cultural institutions, University Circle is a hub for education and the arts. The Cleveland Museum of Art, Cleveland Orchestra, and Case Western Reserve University are all located here.

Shaker Heights: Known for its tree-lined streets and historic homes, Shaker Heights is a suburban community with a strong sense of community and an excellent school system. It's also known for the rapid transit system, the RTA Green Line.

Lakewood: Located just west of Cleveland, Lakewood offers a mix of historic homes, parks, and a thriving commercial district along Detroit Avenue. It has a diverse population and a lively nightlife scene.

Food

Pierogies: Cleveland has a strong Eastern European heritage, and pierogies are a beloved local dish. These dumplings are typically filled with ingredients like potato, cheese, sauerkraut, or meat and are often served with sour cream and onions.

Polish and Eastern European Cuisine: In addition to pierogies, you can explore other Eastern European dishes like kielbasa (sausage), cabbage rolls, and schnitzel at various restaurants and markets in the city.

Cleveland-style Pizza: Cleveland has its own style of pizza, which is characterized by a thick, doughy crust and plenty of cheese and toppings. Try a local pizzeria for a taste of this unique pizza style.

Corned Beef Sandwiches: Corned beef sandwiches, often piled high with tender slices of corned beef, are a staple in many Cleveland delis. Some famous delis in the city serve mouthwatering corned beef sandwiches.

City's Seafood: Being located near Lake Erie, Cleveland offers a variety of fresh seafood options. Lake Erie perch and walleye are local favorites, often served fried or grilled.

Ethnic Cuisine: Cleveland's culinary scene is diverse, with a range of ethnic restaurants offering cuisine from around the world. You can explore flavors from Italy, Greece, India, Vietnam, and more.

Craft Beer: Cleveland has a thriving craft beer scene, with numerous breweries offering a wide selection of locally brewed beers. Pair your beer with some pub grub at one of the city's brewpubs.

Farm-to-Table and Gourmet Dining: The city also boasts upscale dining options, with restaurants focusing on farm-to-table ingredients and gourmet cuisine. These establishments offer creative and seasonal menus.

Travel to Cleveland Ohio

Here are our ten favorite restaurant recommendations!

1. Lola Bistro: Chef Michael Symon's Lola Bistro in downtown Cleveland offers a menu that combines locally sourced ingredients with bold flavors. It's known for its creative American cuisine.

2. The Greenhouse Tavern: A farm-to-table restaurant in downtown Cleveland, The Greenhouse Tavern, offers an inventive menu featuring sustainable and locally sourced ingredients. Their focus on sustainability and innovative dishes has earned them recognition.

3. Dante: Dante Boccuzzi's eponymous restaurant, Dante, is known for its upscale Italian and contemporary American cuisine. It has a sophisticated atmosphere and a diverse menu.

4. Mabel's BBQ: Another venture by Chef Michael Symon, Mabel's BBQ, serves up delicious barbecue dishes with a Cleveland twist. The restaurant is famous for its smoked meats and inventive sides.

5. Crop Bistro: Located in a historic bank building, Crop Bistro offers a unique dining experience. The restaurant specializes in American cuisine with an emphasis on fresh, seasonal ingredients.

6. Sokolowski's University Inn: This family-owned restaurant is a Cleveland institution, serving hearty Polish and Eastern European comfort food. It's known for its pierogies, kielbasa, and classic dishes.

7.Pier W: Perched on the shores of Lake Erie, Pier W offers stunning views and a seafood-focused menu. It's renowned for its fresh seafood offerings and upscale dining experience.

8.L'Albatros Brasserie: Located in an elegant historic building, L'Albatros Brasserie offers French-inspired cuisine in a charming setting. The menu features classic French dishes with a modern twist.

9.Blue Point Grille: Known for its seafood and upscale dining experience, Blue Point Grille offers a menu featuring fresh seafood from around the world. It's a great choice for seafood enthusiasts.

10.Superior Pho: For lovers of Vietnamese cuisine, Superior Pho is a popular choice. It's known for its authentic Vietnamese dishes, including pho, banh mi, and fresh spring rolls.

Travel to Cleveland Ohio

Nightlife

East 4th Street: A bustling entertainment district in downtown Cleveland, known for its restaurants, bars, and nightlife options.

The Flats: A waterfront entertainment district along the Cuyahoga River, offering a mix of bars, clubs, and restaurants.

West 25th Street (Ohio City): Ohio City, just west of downtown, features a lively nightlife scene with craft breweries, cocktail bars, and restaurants.

Warehouse District: Located downtown, this district offers a range of bars, clubs, and lounges, making it a popular nightlife destination.

Tremont: Tremont's historic streets are home to a variety of bars, pubs, and restaurants, creating a vibrant evening atmosphere.

Coventry Village: In the Cleveland Heights neighborhood, Coventry Village has a diverse selection of bars, music venues, and late-night eateries.

Hingetown: Located in Ohio City, Hingetown features trendy bars and an artistic atmosphere, making it a unique nightlife destination.

Gordon Square Arts District: This district offers a mix of bars and theaters, providing options for both entertainment and nightlife.

Playhouse Square: After a show at Playhouse Square, you can explore nearby bars and restaurants for a post-show drink or meal.

University Circle: The area around University Circle has some upscale dining options, ideal for a more refined evening out.

These areas and venues offer a wide range of nightlife experiences, from lively bars and clubs to relaxed lounges and late-night dining options, catering to various tastes and preferences.

Local Traditions & Customs

Polish and Eastern European Heritage: Cleveland has a strong Eastern European heritage, particularly of Polish and Slovak communities. You can find traditions like Pierogi festivals and Dyngus Day celebrations, where locals celebrate with Polish food, music, and cultural events.

Sports Fandom: Clevelanders are known for their passionate support of their sports teams, including the Cleveland Browns (NFL), Cleveland Cavaliers (NBA), and Cleveland Guardians (MLB). Game days often involve tailgating and spirited cheering for the home team.

Polka Music and Dance: Polka music and dance have a strong presence in Cleveland's cultural scene. You can find Polka events and dance clubs where people enjoy traditional Eastern European music and dance.

Lake Erie and Boating: Given its proximity to Lake Erie, boating and water-related activities are popular traditions in Cleveland. Many residents and visitors enjoy boating, fishing, and swimming in the lake during the warmer months.

Cleveland Orchestra: The Cleveland Orchestra, founded in 1918, is one of the city's cultural treasures. It has a rich history of world-class performances and is a source of civic pride.

Cleveland Museum of Art: The Cleveland Museum of Art is renowned for its collection of art spanning various cultures and time periods. Visiting the museum is a cultural tradition for many locals.

West Side Market: The West Side Market is a historic public market in Ohio City, where locals and visitors can purchase fresh produce, meats, and ethnic foods. It's a tradition for many to shop at this iconic market.

Travel to Cleveland Ohio

What to buy?

Cleveland Sports Merchandise: Show your support for Cleveland's sports teams by purchasing merchandise such as jerseys, caps, or T-shirts featuring the Cleveland Browns (NFL), Cleveland Cavaliers (NBA), or Cleveland Guardians (MLB).

Rock and Roll Hall of Fame Memorabilia: The Rock and Roll Hall of Fame in Cleveland has an excellent gift shop with a wide range of music-related items, including T-shirts, posters, and memorabilia from famous musicians.

Local Craft Beer: Cleveland has a thriving craft beer scene, so consider picking up some locally brewed beers or merchandise from one of the city's many breweries.

Pierogi and Eastern European Foods: Cleveland has a strong Eastern European heritage, so you can find delicious pierogi, kielbasa, and other Eastern European food products in local markets. These can make for a unique culinary souvenir.

Local Art and Crafts: Explore the local art scene by visiting galleries and artisan markets. You may find handmade jewelry, ceramics, paintings, and other unique artworks created by local artists.

West Side Market Finds: The West Side Market in Ohio City is a historic market with vendors selling a wide range of fresh foods, spices, and local products. You can find items like artisanal cheese, ethnic foods, and spices.

People Who Know Publishing

Finally, here are the five most famous people from the city!

1.LeBron James: Born in Akron, Ohio, which is part of the Greater Cleveland area, LeBron James is one of the most famous and accomplished basketball players in the world. He played for the Cleveland Cavaliers and led the team to an NBA championship in 2016.

2.Bob Hope: The legendary comedian and entertainer Bob Hope was born in Eltham, London, but his family moved to Cleveland when he was a young boy. He became one of the most iconic figures in the history of American entertainment.

3.Halle Berry: Academy Award-winning actress Halle Berry was born in Cleveland. She has had a successful career in film and is known for her roles in movies like "Monster's Ball" and "X-Men."

4.Drew Carey: Comedian and actor Drew Carey, known for his sitcom "The Drew Carey Show" and hosting "Whose Line Is It Anyway?" and "The Price Is Right," was born and raised in Cleveland.

5.Langston Hughes: The renowned poet, playwright, and social activist Langston Hughes spent a significant part of his childhood and adolescence in Cleveland. He became a central figure in the Harlem Renaissance, contributing significantly to American literature and culture.

Travel to Cleveland Ohio

101+ things to do in the city

1. Visit the Rock and Roll Hall of Fame.
2. Explore the Cleveland Museum of Art.
3. Take a stroll through the Cleveland Botanical Garden.
4. Attend a concert at the Blossom Music Center.
5. Catch a Cleveland Indians baseball game.
6. Cheer on the Cleveland Cavaliers at a basketball game.
7. Attend a Cleveland Browns football game.
8. Visit the Cleveland Metroparks Zoo.
9. Explore the Cleveland Museum of Natural History.
10. Take a cruise on the Goodtime III.
11. Visit the Great Lakes Science Center.
12. Explore the Cleveland Cultural Gardens.
13. Attend a performance at Playhouse Square.
14. Explore the Western Reserve Historical Society.
15. Go for a hike in the Cuyahoga Valley National Park.
16. Visit the Cleveland Aquarium.
17. Explore the USS Cod Submarine Memorial.
18. Discover the Lake View Cemetery.
19. Attend the Cleveland International Film Festival.
20. Take a ride on the Cuyahoga Valley Scenic Railroad.
21. Explore the West Side Market.
22. Attend a Cleveland Orchestra performance at Severance Hall.
23. Visit the A Christmas Story House and Museum.
24. Explore the Cleveland Grays Armory Museum.
25. Explore the Crawford Auto-Aviation Museum.
26. Go to the Great Lakes Brewing Company for a brewery tour.
27. Attend the Cleveland International Piano Competition.
28. Explore the Children's Museum of Cleveland.
29. Go fishing on Lake Erie.
30. Take a yoga class at the Cleveland Yoga Studio.
31. Visit the International Women's Air and Space Museum.
32. Explore the Cleveland Police Museum.
33. Attend the Cleveland Asian Festival.
34. Take a tour of the James A. Garfield National Historic Site.
35. Explore the Dittrick Medical History Center.
36. Attend the Cleveland Garlic Festival.
37. Go birdwatching at the Lake Erie Nature & Science Center.
38. Visit the Maltz Museum of Jewish Heritage.
39. Attend the Cleveland Comedy Festival.
40. Explore the Ukrainian Museum-Archives.

People Who Know Publishing

41. Go ice skating at the Cleveland Foundation Skating Rink.
42. Visit the NASA Glenn Research Center.
43. Explore the Dunham Tavern Museum.
44. Attend the Cleveland National Air Show.
45. Go kayaking on the Cuyahoga River.
46. Visit the Baseball Heritage Museum.
47. Explore the Greater Cleveland Aquarium.
48. Attend a performance at the Beck Center for the Arts.
49. Take a ride on the Euclid Beach Park Grand Carousel.
50. Visit the Cleveland Police Historical Society and Museum.
51. Attend the Cleveland International Tattoo.
52. Explore the Soldiers' and Sailors' Monument.
53. Visit the Dittrick Medical History Center.
54. Attend the Feast of the Assumption in Little Italy.
55. Explore the Cleveland Skating Club.
56. Take a tour of the Federal Reserve Bank of Cleveland.
57. Attend the Tri-C JazzFest.
58. Go to a Cleveland Monsters hockey game.
59. Visit the William G. Mather Museum.
60. Explore the Warther Museum and Gardens.
61. Attend the Cleveland Pride Parade and Festival.
62. Visit the Cleveland Hungarian Heritage Society.
63. Go to a Cleveland Gladiators arena football game.
64. Explore the Ukrainian Museum-Archives.
65. Attend the Cleveland Kurentovanje Festival.
66. Take a scenic drive along the Lake Erie Coastal Ohio Trail.
67. Go horseback riding in the Metroparks.
68. Visit the Dittrick Medical History Center.
69. Attend the Cleveland Museum of Natural History's Think & Drink series.
70. Explore the Italian Cultural Garden.
71. Take a cooking class at the Loretta Paganini School of Cooking.
72. Visit the Cleveland Hungarian Heritage Museum.
73. Attend the Cleveland Labor Day Oktoberfest.
74. Explore the Estonian Cultural Garden.
75. Go ziplining at Common Ground Canopy Tours.
76. Visit the American Police Motorcycle Museum.
77. Explore the Slavic Village neighborhood.
78. Attend the Serbian Cultural Garden's Serbian Festival.
79. Take a scenic drive along the Covered Bridge Tour Route.
80. Visit the Greater Cleveland Aquarium's 230,000-gallon shark exhibit.
81. Attend the Cleveland One World Festival.

Travel to Cleveland Ohio

82. Explore the Slovenian Museum and Archives.
83. Go on a wine tour of Ohio's wine country.
84. Visit the Playhouse Square chandelier.
85. Attend the Great Lakes Burning River Fest.
86. Explore the Irish Cultural Garden.
87. Take a pottery or ceramics class at the Cleveland Institute of Art.
88. Attend the Cleveland Tall Ships Festival.
89. Visit the Greater Cleveland Film Commission.
90. Explore the Arabic Cultural Garden.
91. Go sailing on Lake Erie.
92. Attend the Cleveland Whiskey Festival.
93. Visit the Cleveland Firefighters Memorial.
94. Explore the Shakespeare Garden.
95. Attend the Brite Winter Festival.
96. Take a ride on the Lolly the Trolley tour.
97. Visit the "Free Stamp" sculpture.
98. Attend the Cleveland Asian Lantern Festival.
99. Explore the Ariel Pearl Center.
100. Go on a Cleveland Brewery Tour.
101. Visit the Nature Center at Shaker Lakes.
102. Attend the Cleveland Dragon Boat Festival.
103. Explore the Rockefeller Park Greenhouse.
104. Take a scenic drive along the Ohio & Erie Canal Towpath Trail.
105. Visit the Cleveland Pops Orchestra.
106. Attend a performance at the Near West Theatre.
107. Explore the Cultural Gardens at Wade Oval.
108. Go paddleboarding on the Cuyahoga River.
109. Attend the Feast of St. Augustine in Tremont.
110. Visit the Cleveland Pickle.

1. Visit the Rock and Roll Hall of Fame.

Visiting the Rock and Roll Hall of Fame in Cleveland is a must for music enthusiasts and fans of rock and roll history. Here's what you can expect:

The Rock and Roll Hall of Fame is a world-renowned museum and cultural institution dedicated to preserving the history and celebrating the influence of rock and roll music. It's located on the shores of Lake Erie in downtown Cleveland, Ohio. The museum's distinctive design, featuring a glass pyramid and sleek architecture, makes it a prominent landmark along the waterfront.

Inside, you'll find a vast collection of artifacts, memorabilia, and exhibits that tell the story of rock and roll, from its roots to the present day. Here are some highlights:

Exhibits: The museum features a rotating collection of exhibits that showcase the evolution of rock and roll, its iconic artists, and the cultural impact of the genre. These exhibits often include rare instruments, costumes, handwritten lyrics, and multimedia presentations.

Hall of Fame Inductees: The heart of the museum is the Hall of Fame itself, which honors the most influential musicians, bands, producers, and other industry professionals who have made significant contributions to rock and roll. You can explore the exhibits dedicated to these inductees.

Interactive Experiences: The Rock and Roll Hall of Fame offers interactive displays and experiences, allowing visitors to engage with the music. You can listen to classic songs, play musical instruments, and even step into a recording studio.

Concerts and Events: The museum hosts live concerts, film screenings, lectures, and special events throughout the year. Check the museum's calendar for upcoming performances and programs.

Gift Shop: The museum's gift shop offers a wide range of rock and roll-themed merchandise, including T-shirts, posters, music, and collectibles.

Café and Dining: The All Access Café inside the museum offers a selection of food and beverages, making it a convenient place to grab a bite during your visit.

Travel to Cleveland Ohio

Scenic Views: Don't miss the opportunity to enjoy scenic views of Lake Erie and the Cleveland skyline from the museum's outdoor plaza.

Visiting the Rock and Roll Hall of Fame is not only an opportunity to learn about the history of rock music but also a chance to be inspired by the creativity and passion of the artists who have shaped the genre. Whether you're a lifelong fan or just curious about the world of rock and roll, the museum offers an immersive and educational experience.

2. Explore the Cleveland Museum of Art.

Exploring the Cleveland Museum of Art is a delightful and enriching experience for art enthusiasts and visitors interested in a diverse range of artistic styles and cultures. Here's what you can expect when you visit:

Collection: The Cleveland Museum of Art is renowned for its extensive and diverse collection of artworks that span thousands of years and multiple cultures. The collection includes art from ancient civilizations, European and American paintings, Asian and African art, contemporary pieces, and much more.

Highlights:

The Armor Court: One of the museum's most iconic spaces, the Armor Court features an impressive collection of armor and weaponry from different time periods and regions.
European and American Art: Explore a wide array of European and American paintings, sculptures, and decorative arts. The museum boasts works by famous artists like Monet, Van Gogh, and Rodin.
Asian Art: The museum's Asian art collection is extensive, featuring Chinese, Japanese, Korean, and Indian artworks, including stunning porcelain, textiles, and sculptures.
African and Ancient American Art: Discover the art and artifacts of African and Ancient American cultures, including masks, textiles, and pottery.
Contemporary Art: The contemporary art section showcases works by modern artists, providing insight into the evolving world of art.
Special Exhibitions: The museum hosts rotating special exhibitions, which offer fresh perspectives on various art forms, time periods, or themes. These exhibitions often bring in artworks from other institutions and private collections.

Interactive Experiences: The museum offers interactive exhibits and activities, making it engaging for visitors of all ages. These may include touch screens, digital guides, and hands-on art-making experiences.

Lecture Series and Events: The museum regularly hosts lectures, workshops, and events related to art and culture. Check the museum's calendar for upcoming programs.

Garden and Outdoor Spaces: Don't miss the beautiful Wade Park and the Fine Arts Garden surrounding the museum. It's a serene place to relax and appreciate sculptures and landscaping.

Dining: The museum has on-site dining options, including the Provenance Café and Provenance Restaurant, where you can enjoy a meal or a snack during your visit.

Gift Shop: The museum's gift shop offers a wide range of art-inspired items, books, jewelry, and unique gifts.

Accessibility: The museum is committed to providing accessibility to all visitors. It offers services like wheelchairs, assistive listening devices, and guided tours for individuals with disabilities.

Admission: While general admission to the museum is free, there may be fees for special exhibitions and programs. It's a good idea to check the museum's website for up-to-date information on hours of operation, admission fees, and any special exhibitions.

Visiting the Cleveland Museum of Art is not just an opportunity to view incredible artworks but also a chance to immerse yourself in the rich history of human creativity and expression from around the world. Whether you're a seasoned art enthusiast or a first-time visitor, the museum offers a world-class cultural experience.

Travel to Cleveland Ohio

3. Take a stroll through the Cleveland Botanical Garden.

Taking a stroll through the Cleveland Botanical Garden is a delightful and serene experience, offering a beautiful escape into the world of plants, flowers, and nature. Here's what you can expect when you visit:

Outdoor Gardens:

Hershey Children's Garden: Designed for young visitors, this garden encourages hands-on exploration and play with features like a treehouse and splash garden.
Japanese Garden: Designed in the Japanese tradition, this garden features tranquil water features, meticulously pruned plants, and stone pathways.
Rose Garden: The Rose Garden showcases a stunning array of roses, providing a colorful and fragrant backdrop for your stroll.
Perennial Garden: Featuring a variety of perennial plants, this garden offers seasonal displays of flowers, foliage, and textures.
Glasshouse:

The Eleanor Armstrong Smith Glasshouse is a highlight of the botanical garden. It's a massive glass conservatory that houses a range of exotic plants from different climates, including a tropical rainforest and a desert environment.
Inside the Glasshouse, you'll encounter waterfalls, exotic flora, and even wildlife like butterflies and birds. The Glasshouse is divided into distinct biomes, each representing a different part of the world.
Special Exhibitions: The botanical garden often hosts rotating special exhibitions and displays that highlight specific plant collections, art installations, or educational themes. Check the garden's website for information on current exhibitions.

Events and Programs: The Cleveland Botanical Garden offers a variety of events and programs throughout the year, including workshops, plant sales, garden tours, and educational programs for all ages.

Garden Store: The Garden Store at the botanical garden is a great place to shop for gardening tools, books, plants, and unique gifts related to horticulture and nature.

Dining: The Garden Café offers a pleasant spot to enjoy a meal or a snack amid the greenery. The menu often features fresh and locally sourced ingredients.

Educational Opportunities: The garden is committed to education and offers a range of programs for students, teachers, and adults interested in learning more about plants, gardening, and ecology.

Accessibility: The botanical garden is designed to be accessible to visitors of all abilities, with pathways and amenities to accommodate wheelchairs and strollers.

Hours and Admission: Be sure to check the garden's website for current hours of operation and admission fees, as they may vary by season and age group.

Visiting the Cleveland Botanical Garden is a wonderful way to connect with the natural world, appreciate the beauty of diverse plant species, and find inspiration for your own gardening endeavors. Whether you're a seasoned botanist or simply seeking a peaceful outdoor experience, the garden provides a tranquil and educational setting for all visitors.

4. Attend a concert at the Blossom Music Center.

Attending a concert at the Blossom Music Center is a memorable experience, especially for music lovers. Here's what you can expect when you attend a concert at this iconic outdoor amphitheater:

Outdoor Venue: The Blossom Music Center is an open-air amphitheater located in Cuyahoga Falls, Ohio, about 25 miles north of downtown Cleveland. The venue is situated within a scenic natural setting, surrounded by woodlands and greenery.

Seating Options: The venue offers a range of seating options to suit different preferences and budgets. These include covered pavilion seating with reserved and lawn seating, which allows concertgoers to bring their own blankets or low-backed lawn chairs.

Diverse Concerts: Blossom hosts a wide variety of concerts and live music events throughout the year, featuring an eclectic lineup of artists and genres. From classical performances by the Cleveland Orchestra to rock, pop, country, and more, there's something for everyone.

Travel to Cleveland Ohio

Tailgating: Many concertgoers enjoy tailgating in the parking lots before shows, creating a lively and communal atmosphere. Be sure to check the venue's policies regarding tailgating and parking.

Acoustics: The Blossom Music Center is renowned for its excellent acoustics and natural sound quality. The pavilion offers exceptional sound clarity, and the hillside lawn seating provides a more casual and relaxed concert experience.

Scenic Views: The amphitheater's location within the Cuyahoga Valley National Park provides stunning natural surroundings. Concertgoers can enjoy beautiful views, especially during evening performances as the sun sets.

Food and Beverages: The venue has concession stands offering a variety of food and drink options, including classic concert fare like hot dogs, hamburgers, and beverages. You can also bring your own picnic, but be sure to check the venue's policies on outside food and drink.

Parking: The Blossom Music Center provides ample parking facilities. Depending on your ticket and the show, you may have different parking options, so it's a good idea to check in advance.

Arrival and Departure: Arrive early to allow time for parking and finding your seats. After the concert, expect some traffic as you exit the venue, so plan accordingly.

Weather: Since the venue is outdoors, it's advisable to check the weather forecast and be prepared for various conditions. Consider bringing sunscreen, rain gear, or a light jacket depending on the season.

Ticketing: Tickets for concerts at Blossom Music Center can be purchased through the venue's website, authorized ticketing platforms, or in person at the box office.

Attending a concert at the Blossom Music Center offers the chance to enjoy live music in a beautiful natural setting. Whether you're a fan of classical music, rock, or any other genre, the venue's diverse lineup ensures a memorable musical experience.

5. Catch a Cleveland Indians baseball game.

Watching a Cleveland Indians baseball game is a classic American pastime and a fantastic way to immerse yourself in the city's sports culture. Here's what you can expect when you attend a Cleveland Indians game:

Team: The Cleveland Indians are a Major League Baseball (MLB) team based in Cleveland, Ohio. The team is a member of the American League (AL) Central Division.

Ballpark: The Indians play their home games at Progressive Field, which is located in downtown Cleveland. The ballpark offers a modern and fan-friendly experience while preserving the charm of traditional baseball.

Game Day Atmosphere: Attending a baseball game at Progressive Field is not just about the sport; it's about the entire experience. You'll find a lively atmosphere with passionate fans, ballpark food, music, and entertainment.

Seating Options: Progressive Field offers a range of seating options, including lower-level seats, upper-level seats, suites, and special seating areas. Whether you prefer to be close to the action or enjoy a higher vantage point, you'll find a seat that suits your preferences and budget.

Food and Drinks: Ballpark cuisine is a highlight of the experience. You can savor classic baseball fare like hot dogs, nachos, and peanuts, as well as a variety of local and gourmet food options. Be sure to try some Cleveland specialties.

Fan Activities: The ballpark features interactive fan areas, including the Kids Clubhouse and the Right Field District, where you can enjoy games, activities, and socializing with fellow fans.

Merchandise: The team's official store, the Indians Team Shop, offers a wide selection of merchandise, including jerseys, caps, T-shirts, and memorabilia.

Mascot: Keep an eye out for the Indians' mascot, Slider, who often interacts with fans and adds to the fun.

Special Events: The Indians occasionally host special events during games, such as fireworks nights, giveaways, and themed nights. Check the team's schedule for any upcoming promotions.

Tickets: Tickets for Cleveland Indians games can be purchased online through the team's official website, at the Progressive Field box office, or through authorized ticketing platforms.

Game Schedule: MLB has a regular season that typically runs from spring to early autumn. Be sure to check the team's schedule for upcoming games and promotions.

Attending a Cleveland Indians baseball game is not only about watching America's favorite pastime but also about experiencing the camaraderie and excitement of live sports. Whether you're a die-hard baseball fan or just looking for a fun and entertaining outing, a trip to Progressive Field is sure to provide a memorable time in Cleveland.

6. Cheer on the Cleveland Cavaliers at a basketball game.

Cheering on the Cleveland Cavaliers at a basketball game is an exhilarating experience for sports enthusiasts. Here's what you can expect when attending a Cleveland Cavaliers game:

Team: The Cleveland Cavaliers, often referred to as the Cavs, are a professional basketball team based in Cleveland, Ohio. They compete in the National Basketball Association (NBA) as a member of the Central Division in the Eastern Conference.

Arena: The Cavaliers play their home games at the Rocket Mortgage FieldHouse, which is located in downtown Cleveland. The arena offers state-of-the-art facilities and a vibrant game-day atmosphere.

Game Day Excitement: A Cavaliers game day is filled with excitement, starting from the moment you arrive at the arena. Fans gather early to tailgate, enjoy live music, and participate in pre-game festivities.

Seating Options: The Rocket Mortgage FieldHouse offers a variety of seating options to suit different preferences and budgets. You can choose from lower-level seats, upper-level seats, suites, and even premium club seating.

Entertainment: In addition to the basketball action, Cavaliers games feature entertainment elements such as halftime shows, mascot appearances (including Moondog and Sir C.C.), and crowd-engaging activities to keep fans entertained.

Food and Drinks: The arena boasts a diverse array of dining options, including traditional stadium fare like hot dogs and nachos, as well as local Cleveland cuisine and craft beer options.

Fan Zone: The "Cavs Fan Zone" is an interactive area inside the arena where fans can enjoy games, photo opportunities, and interactive experiences before and after the game.

Team Shop: The Cavaliers Team Shop is your go-to destination for official team merchandise, including jerseys, hats, apparel, and collectibles.

Special Events: The team occasionally hosts special events during games, such as theme nights, giveaways, and promotions. Check the Cavaliers' schedule for any upcoming events.

Tickets: Tickets for Cleveland Cavaliers games can be purchased online through the team's official website, at the Rocket Mortgage FieldHouse box office, or through authorized ticketing platforms.

NBA Season: The NBA season typically runs from late October to April, with playoffs extending into the spring and early summer. Be sure to check the Cavaliers' schedule for upcoming games.

Attending a Cleveland Cavaliers basketball game is an opportunity to witness high-level athleticism, enjoy the camaraderie of fellow fans, and immerse yourself in the excitement of professional basketball. Whether you're a dedicated basketball enthusiast or just looking for an energetic and thrilling night out, a Cavaliers game at Rocket Mortgage FieldHouse delivers an unforgettable sports experience.

7. Attend a Cleveland Browns football game.

Attending a Cleveland Browns football game is an electrifying experience, especially for football fans. Here's what you can expect when you attend a Cleveland Browns game:

Travel to Cleveland Ohio

Team: The Cleveland Browns are a professional football team based in Cleveland, Ohio, competing in the National Football League (NFL) as a member of the American Football Conference (AFC) North Division.

Stadium: The Browns play their home games at FirstEnergy Stadium, which is located on the shores of Lake Erie in downtown Cleveland. The stadium offers a great view of the city skyline and the lake.

Game Day Atmosphere: A Browns game day is marked by a lively and passionate atmosphere. The "Dawg Pound" section in the stadium is known for its enthusiastic and dedicated fans, creating an unforgettable environment.

Seating Options: FirstEnergy Stadium offers a range of seating options, including lower-level seats, upper-level seats, suites, and club seating. You can choose the seating that best fits your preferences and budget.

Tailgating: Tailgating is a beloved tradition among Browns fans. Parking lots around the stadium are filled with fans cooking up barbecue, playing games, and celebrating before the game.

Food and Drinks: Inside the stadium, you can enjoy a variety of game-day food, including classic stadium fare like hot dogs, pretzels, and nachos. Local Cleveland cuisine is also available, as well as craft beers.

Entertainment: Browns games feature entertainment elements, including the Dawg Pound, mascot appearances (including Chomps), halftime shows, and crowd-engaging activities to keep fans excited.

Team Shop: The Browns Team Shop offers a wide range of official team merchandise, including jerseys, hats, apparel, and memorabilia.

Special Events: The team occasionally hosts special events during games, such as theme days, giveaways, and promotions. Check the Browns' schedule for any upcoming events.

Tickets: Tickets for Cleveland Browns games can be purchased online through the team's official website, at the FirstEnergy Stadium box office, or through authorized ticketing platforms.

NFL Season: The NFL season typically starts in early September and runs through the regular season until late December or early January, with playoff games extending into January and February. Be sure to check the Browns' schedule for upcoming games.

Attending a Cleveland Browns football game is a fantastic way to embrace the excitement of the NFL, immerse yourself in the enthusiasm of dedicated fans, and enjoy the thrill of live football action. Whether you're a lifelong fan or just looking for a thrilling sports experience, a Browns game at FirstEnergy Stadium promises an unforgettable time in Cleveland.

8. Visit the Cleveland Metroparks Zoo.

Visiting the Cleveland Metroparks Zoo is a fun and educational experience for individuals and families. Here's what you can expect when you explore this popular attraction:

Zoo Layout: The Cleveland Metroparks Zoo is situated on 183 acres in Cleveland's Big Creek Valley and features a wide variety of animals from around the world. The zoo is divided into several themed areas and exhibits, making it easy to navigate and explore.

Animal Exhibits: The zoo is home to over 3,000 animals representing more than 600 species. You can expect to see animals from all corners of the globe, including mammals, birds, reptiles, amphibians, and fish. Some of the popular exhibits include the RainForest, African Savanna, Australian Adventure, Northern Trek, and Primate, Cat & Aquatics Building.

Conservation and Education: The Cleveland Metroparks Zoo is dedicated to conservation and education. Throughout the zoo, you'll find informative signage and interactive displays that provide insights into the animals, their habitats, and conservation efforts to protect endangered species.

Interactive Experiences: The zoo offers various interactive experiences, including animal encounters, feedings, and educational programs. These opportunities allow visitors to get up close with certain animals and learn more about their behaviors and care.

Naturalistic Habitats: Many of the animal exhibits at the zoo are designed to replicate natural habitats as closely as possible. This provides a more enriching and educational experience for visitors while ensuring the well-being of the animals.

Play Areas: The zoo has designated play areas for children, including a splash pad and a playground. These areas offer a break for kids to expend energy and have some fun.

Food and Dining: You'll find dining options within the zoo, including cafés and snack stands where you can grab a meal or a snack during your visit.

Gift Shop: The zoo's gift shop offers a variety of souvenirs, toys, and animal-themed merchandise.

Events and Programs: Throughout the year, the zoo hosts special events, educational programs, and seasonal celebrations. Check the zoo's website for information on current events and programs.

Accessibility: The zoo strives to be accessible to all visitors, including those with disabilities. Wheelchairs and strollers are available for rent.

Hours and Admission: Be sure to check the zoo's website for current hours of operation, admission fees, and any special promotions or discounts.

Visiting the Cleveland Metroparks Zoo is an opportunity to connect with wildlife, learn about conservation efforts, and enjoy a day of outdoor exploration. Whether you're a nature enthusiast, a family with children, or simply looking for an enjoyable outing, the zoo offers a memorable experience for visitors of all ages.

9. Explore the Cleveland Museum of Natural History.

Exploring the Cleveland Museum of Natural History offers visitors the opportunity to delve into the fascinating world of natural science and discovery. Here's what you can expect when you visit:

Exhibits: The museum features a wide range of exhibits that cover various aspects of natural history, including paleontology, geology, astronomy, anthropology, and biology. Some notable exhibits include:

Dinosaur Hall: Explore the world of dinosaurs with a collection of fossils and life-sized dinosaur reconstructions.

Perkins Wildlife Center & Woods Garden: Encounter live animals native to Ohio, including birds of prey and mammals, in a natural outdoor setting.

Human Origins Gallery: Learn about human evolution and the history of our species.

Mineral and Gem Collection: Marvel at a stunning collection of minerals, gemstones, and meteorites.

Astronomy: Explore the cosmos in the Shafran Planetarium and Ralph Mueller Observatory.

Planetarium: The Shafran Planetarium at the museum offers a range of astronomy programs, including star shows and full-dome movies. It's a great place to learn about the night sky and the universe.

Educational Programs: The museum offers a variety of educational programs for visitors of all ages. These may include workshops, lectures, and hands-on activities related to natural history and science.

Sankofa African American Heritage Museum: This museum within a museum focuses on African American history and culture, featuring exhibitions, art, and artifacts that explore the African American experience in Cleveland and beyond.

Archaeological Collections: The museum houses extensive collections of archaeological artifacts, including those from Ohio's prehistoric and historic Native American cultures.

Botanical Garden: The outdoor Judith and Maynard H. Murch IV Plant Science Center features beautiful gardens and plant collections, providing a tranquil space to explore nature.

Gift Shop: The museum's gift shop offers a range of science-themed books, educational toys, and unique gifts.

Accessibility: The museum strives to be accessible to all visitors, including those with disabilities. Wheelchairs are available for use, and the facility is equipped with ramps and elevators.

Hours and Admission: Check the museum's website for current hours of operation, admission fees, and any special exhibitions or events.

Visiting the Cleveland Museum of Natural History is a journey through the natural world, offering a wealth of knowledge, interactive experiences, and the opportunity to appreciate the wonders of science and our planet's history.

Travel to Cleveland Ohio

Whether you're a science enthusiast, a student, or simply curious about the world around you, the museum provides a captivating and educational experience for visitors of all backgrounds.

10. Take a cruise on the Goodtime III.

Taking a cruise on the Goodtime III is a relaxing and scenic way to experience the beauty of Cleveland from Lake Erie. Here's what you can expect when you embark on this cruise:

Cruise Overview: The Goodtime III is the largest excursion ship on the Great Lakes and offers a variety of cruise options for visitors. It departs from the North Coast Harbor in downtown Cleveland and provides breathtaking views of the city skyline and Lake Erie.

Types of Cruises: The Goodtime III offers several types of cruises to suit different preferences:

Sightseeing Cruises: These cruises provide a narrated tour of the Cleveland waterfront, highlighting landmarks, historical sites, and interesting facts about the city. It's an excellent way to learn about Cleveland's history and see its iconic skyline.

Lunch and Dinner Cruises: Enjoy a meal while cruising on Lake Erie. Lunch and dinner cruises typically include a buffet-style meal, entertainment, and scenic views.

Specialty Cruises: The Goodtime III offers specialty cruises for various occasions, such as holiday-themed cruises, wine-tasting cruises, and live music events. Be sure to check the cruise schedule for any upcoming special events.

Amenities: The ship is equipped with amenities to enhance your cruise experience. You'll find comfortable indoor and outdoor seating, restrooms, a full-service bar, and a dance floor on board.

Scenic Views: As you cruise along Lake Erie, you'll have the opportunity to take in stunning views of the Cleveland skyline, including landmarks like the Rock and Roll Hall of Fame, FirstEnergy Stadium (home of the Cleveland Browns), and the historic bridges spanning the Cuyahoga River.

Narration: Most sightseeing cruises offer informative narration, providing historical context and interesting facts about the city and its waterfront attractions.

Photography: Be sure to bring your camera or smartphone to capture the picturesque views, especially during sunset cruises when the city's lights illuminate the skyline.

Accessibility: The Goodtime III is designed to be accessible to all guests, including those with disabilities. The main deck and restrooms are wheelchair accessible.

Reservations: It's advisable to make reservations for your desired cruise in advance, especially during peak tourist seasons or for specialty cruises.

Duration: The duration of the cruise varies depending on the type of cruise you choose. Sightseeing cruises are typically shorter, while lunch and dinner cruises offer a more extended experience.

Weather: Be prepared for varying weather conditions, as Lake Erie can be breezy and temperatures may differ from the city's inland areas. Dress accordingly and bring layers if needed.

A cruise on the Goodtime III is not only a relaxing and scenic experience but also an opportunity to gain a unique perspective of Cleveland from the water. Whether you're a tourist looking to explore the city or a local wanting to enjoy a leisurely day on the lake, the Goodtime III offers a memorable and enjoyable outing.

11. Visit the Great Lakes Science Center.

Visiting the Great Lakes Science Center in Cleveland is an engaging and educational experience that offers a wide range of interactive exhibits and activities. Here's what you can expect when you explore this science museum:

Exhibits: The Great Lakes Science Center features a variety of hands-on exhibits and displays that cover a broad spectrum of scientific topics. Some highlights include:

Travel to Cleveland Ohio

NASA Glenn Visitor Center: Learn about space exploration, the history of NASA, and the role of the nearby Glenn Research Center in Cleveland.

Science Phenomena: Explore the principles of physics, chemistry, and biology through interactive exhibits that allow you to experiment and observe scientific phenomena.

The Polymer Funhouse: Designed for younger visitors, this exhibit area focuses on the science of polymers, offering fun and educational activities.

Steamship William G. Mather Museum: Tour this restored 1925 steamship, which provides insight into Great Lakes shipping history and maritime engineering.

Cleveland Creates Zone: Engage in engineering and design challenges using a variety of materials, fostering creativity and problem-solving skills.

Dome Theater: The museum's Cleveland Clinic Dome Theater offers immersive experiences with a giant domed screen, where you can watch documentaries and educational films on a wide range of topics, including nature, space, and technology.

Special Exhibits: The museum often hosts rotating special exhibitions that delve into specific scientific themes, offering fresh content and experiences with each visit.

Interactive Activities: Throughout the museum, you'll find interactive activities and demonstrations conducted by knowledgeable staff, making it easy to learn and engage with the exhibits.

Educational Programs: The Great Lakes Science Center offers educational programs, workshops, and camps for students of all ages, making it a popular destination for school field trips.

Accessibility: The museum is committed to providing accessibility for all visitors, including those with disabilities. Wheelchairs are available for use, and the facility is equipped with ramps and elevators.

Food and Dining: The on-site café offers a variety of food and beverage options, making it convenient for visitors to grab a meal or a snack during their visit.

Gift Shop: The museum's gift shop features science-themed toys, books, apparel, and souvenirs, allowing you to take a piece of the museum home with you.

Hours and Admission: Be sure to check the museum's website for current hours of operation, admission fees, and any special exhibitions or events.

Visiting the Great Lakes Science Center is a fantastic way to spark curiosity, explore scientific concepts, and engage in hands-on learning. Whether you're a family with children, a student, or simply curious about the wonders of science and technology, the museum provides an inspiring and interactive environment to satisfy your scientific interests.

12. Explore the Cleveland Cultural Gardens.

Exploring the Cleveland Cultural Gardens is a unique and enriching experience that allows you to celebrate the diversity of cultures and heritage in a beautifully landscaped setting. Here's what you can expect when you visit the Cleveland Cultural Gardens:

Historical Background: The Cleveland Cultural Gardens is a collection of gardens, each dedicated to a specific nationality or culture. It is located in the Rockefeller Park in Cleveland and has a rich history dating back to the early 20th century.

Garden Diversity: As you stroll through the Cultural Gardens, you'll encounter a wide range of garden styles, each inspired by the culture it represents. The gardens showcase a diverse array of plants, sculptures, and architectural elements that reflect the heritage and traditions of various ethnic communities.

Nationality and Culture: Each garden represents a different nationality or culture, often with a unique design and features that reflect the identity and contributions of that group. Some of the cultural gardens you can explore include the Italian, Hebrew, Irish, Greek, Chinese, African American, and many more.

Scenic Walk: The gardens are interconnected by winding pathways, making it possible to take a leisurely walk or bike ride through the entire collection. Along the way, you'll encounter beautiful landscapes and cultural symbols.

Travel to Cleveland Ohio

Sculptures and Monuments: Many of the gardens feature sculptures, monuments, and plaques that pay tribute to prominent individuals, historical events, or cultural achievements related to the respective cultures.

Events and Festivals: The Cleveland Cultural Gardens often host cultural festivals, events, and performances throughout the year, celebrating the traditions, music, dance, and food of various cultures. These events provide an opportunity to immerse yourself in different cultural experiences.

Photography: The Cultural Gardens offer numerous picturesque spots for photography. Whether you're a professional photographer or just want to capture the beauty of the gardens, you'll find ample opportunities for stunning shots.

Peace and Reflection: The gardens provide a serene and peaceful environment for quiet contemplation and reflection. Many visitors find solace and inspiration in the tranquil surroundings.

Accessibility: The pathways are designed to be accessible for visitors of all abilities, including those with disabilities or mobility challenges.

Visitor Center: The Cleveland Cultural Gardens Federation has a visitor center where you can learn more about the history and significance of the gardens.

Guided Tours: Consider taking a guided tour to gain deeper insights into the history, symbolism, and stories behind the individual gardens. Check with the Cultural Gardens Federation for tour availability.

Hours and Access: The Cultural Gardens are generally open to the public year-round, but specific hours of operation may vary by season. Check the official website or contact the Cultural Gardens Federation for the most up-to-date information.

Exploring the Cleveland Cultural Gardens is a journey through cultures, histories, and landscapes, offering a unique opportunity to appreciate the rich tapestry of Cleveland's diverse community. Whether you're interested in horticulture, cultural heritage, or simply enjoying a peaceful outdoor setting, the gardens provide a memorable and educational experience for all visitors.

13. Attend a performance at Playhouse Square.

Attending a performance at Playhouse Square in Cleveland is a cultural experience that showcases a wide range of live entertainment, from Broadway shows and musicals to concerts, plays, and dance performances. Here's what you can expect when you attend a performance at this iconic theater district:

Variety of Venues: Playhouse Square is home to multiple theaters, each with its own unique character and size. Some of the key venues include the KeyBank State Theatre, Connor Palace, Ohio Theatre, Allen Theatre, and the Hanna Theatre. These theaters vary in size, allowing for a diverse lineup of performances.

Broadway Shows: Playhouse Square is known for hosting Broadway touring productions, bringing popular Broadway musicals and plays to Cleveland. These shows feature top-tier talent and high-quality productions, providing a taste of Broadway in the heart of the city.

Concerts and Music: In addition to Broadway shows, Playhouse Square hosts a variety of concerts and musical performances, covering genres such as classical, jazz, rock, pop, and more. Renowned musicians and orchestras often grace the stages here.

Plays and Dramatic Performances: The theater district also features plays, dramas, and performances by local and national theater companies. You can catch classic plays, contemporary dramas, and thought-provoking theatrical works.

Dance Performances: Dance enthusiasts can enjoy a diverse range of dance performances, from classical ballet and contemporary dance to cultural and modern dance forms.

Comedy Shows: Playhouse Square occasionally hosts comedy performances, bringing stand-up comedians and comedic acts to entertain audiences with laughter.

Family-Friendly Shows: Many performances at Playhouse Square are suitable for families and children, making it a great destination for family outings.

Travel to Cleveland Ohio

Art and Architecture: The historic theaters at Playhouse Square boast stunning architecture and decorative elements that add to the ambiance of the performances. Take time to appreciate the beauty of these venues.

Pre-Show Dining: Playhouse Square is surrounded by restaurants and dining options, making it easy to enjoy a meal before or after the performance. Some venues even have on-site dining options.

Accessibility: The theaters at Playhouse Square are committed to providing accessibility for all patrons, including those with disabilities. Wheelchair-accessible seating and facilities are available.

Tickets and Reservations: It's advisable to purchase tickets in advance, especially for popular shows. Tickets can be purchased online through the Playhouse Square website, at the box office, or through authorized ticketing platforms.

Parking: There are parking options in the vicinity of Playhouse Square, including garages and surface lots. Plan your parking in advance, as availability may vary depending on the time of the performance.

Attending a performance at Playhouse Square is a cultural and artistic treat, offering a chance to immerse yourself in the world of live entertainment. Whether you're a theater aficionado, music lover, or simply seeking a memorable night out, Playhouse Square provides a diverse array of performances to suit various tastes and interests.

14. Explore the Western Reserve Historical Society.

Exploring the Western Reserve Historical Society (WRHS) in Cleveland is a journey through the history and heritage of the Western Reserve region of Ohio. Here's what you can expect when you visit this cultural and historical institution:

Museum: The Western Reserve Historical Society operates the Cleveland History Center, which houses a museum with a rich and diverse collection of artifacts, documents, and exhibits that tell the story of Cleveland and the surrounding region.

Exhibits: The museum features a wide range of exhibits, each focusing on different aspects of local history. Some highlights include:

Cleveland Starts Here®: This exhibit provides an engaging introduction to the history of Cleveland and its growth from a frontier town to a major industrial city.

In Grand Style: Explore the history of fashion and clothing in Cleveland, showcasing clothing and accessories from various time periods.

Families at Play: This interactive exhibit takes visitors on a journey through the history of leisure and recreation in Cleveland, from picnics to sports.

Auto Orientations: Learn about the impact of the automobile on Cleveland's society and culture through a collection of historic cars and memorabilia.

Crawford Auto Aviation Collection: This extensive collection showcases automobiles, aircraft, and related items, celebrating the history of transportation.

Crawford Aviation Museum: This dedicated museum within the WRHS focuses on the history of aviation and features an impressive array of aircraft, including historic planes and artifacts.

Research Library: The WRHS houses a research library with a vast collection of documents, manuscripts, photographs, and archives related to the history of Northeast Ohio. Researchers and historians can access these resources for in-depth study and exploration.

Genealogy Resources: If you're interested in tracing your family's roots or genealogy, the WRHS provides access to genealogy databases, records, and expert guidance for genealogical research.

Educational Programs: The WRHS offers educational programs, lectures, workshops, and special events that delve into various aspects of local history, making it a valuable resource for lifelong learners.

Archives: The institution preserves and maintains an extensive collection of historical documents, photographs, and records, making it a valuable resource for historians, researchers, and students.

Accessibility: The WRHS is committed to providing accessibility for all visitors, including those with disabilities. Wheelchair accessibility and facilities are available.

Hours and Admission: Be sure to check the WRHS website for current hours of operation, admission fees, and any special exhibitions or events.

Visiting the Western Reserve Historical Society and the Cleveland History Center is a fascinating journey through time, offering insights into the rich history, culture, and heritage of the Western Reserve region and the city of Cleveland. Whether you're a history enthusiast, a student, or simply curious about the past, the WRHS provides an engaging and educational experience for visitors of all ages.

15. Go for a hike in the Cuyahoga Valley National Park.

Going for a hike in Cuyahoga Valley National Park is a wonderful way to connect with nature and explore the scenic beauty of this protected area in northeastern Ohio. Here's what you can expect when you embark on a hike in Cuyahoga Valley National Park:

Diverse Trails: Cuyahoga Valley National Park offers a wide variety of hiking trails, catering to hikers of all skill levels. Whether you're a novice or an experienced trekker, you'll find trails that suit your preferences and abilities.

Scenic Beauty: The park is known for its picturesque landscapes, including rolling hills, lush forests, waterfalls, and the meandering Cuyahoga River. Each trail offers unique views and natural beauty, making every hike a memorable experience.

Wildlife Viewing: Cuyahoga Valley National Park is home to a diverse range of wildlife, including deer, foxes, beavers, and various bird species. Keep an eye out for opportunities to spot wildlife while hiking.

Trail Lengths: The park's trails vary in length, from short, easy walks to longer, more challenging hikes. Some trails are less than a mile long and are perfect for a quick outing, while others can be several miles in length and may require more time and effort.

Difficulty Levels: Trails in the park are rated for difficulty, so you can choose hikes that match your fitness and skill levels. There are easy, moderate, and strenuous trails available.

Visitor Centers: The park has visitor centers, such as the Boston Store Visitor Center and the Peninsula Depot Visitor Center, where you can obtain trail maps, learn about the park's history and ecology, and get recommendations for hikes.

Trail Maps: Be sure to pick up a trail map or download one from the park's website before heading out on your hike. Having a map will help you navigate the park's extensive trail system.

Seasonal Changes: The park's landscapes change with the seasons, offering unique experiences year-round. Spring and summer bring lush greenery and blooming wildflowers, while fall displays vibrant foliage. Winter provides opportunities for snowshoeing and cross-country skiing on designated trails.

Weather and Clothing: Check the weather forecast before your hike and dress appropriately for the conditions. Wear comfortable hiking shoes, dress in layers, and bring essentials like water, snacks, a hat, and sunscreen.

Leave No Trace: Practice Leave No Trace principles by respecting the park's natural environment. Stay on designated trails, dispose of trash properly, and avoid disturbing wildlife.

Pets: If you plan to hike with pets, be aware of the park's pet regulations, including leash requirements and designated pet-friendly trails.

Park Regulations: Familiarize yourself with park regulations, including park hours, camping rules, and any other specific guidelines related to the trail you plan to hike.

Cuyahoga Valley National Park offers a diverse range of hiking experiences, from leisurely strolls to challenging treks. Whether you're seeking solitude in nature, exploring with family and friends, or simply looking for a healthy outdoor activity, the park's hiking trails provide a perfect opportunity to immerse yourself in the natural beauty of this national park.

Travel to Cleveland Ohio

16. Visit the Cleveland Aquarium.

Visiting the Greater Cleveland Aquarium is a captivating and educational experience that allows you to explore the underwater world and learn about aquatic life. Here's what you can expect when you visit the aquarium:

Aquatic Exhibits: The Greater Cleveland Aquarium features a diverse range of aquatic exhibits, each showcasing different marine habitats and species. Some highlights include:

Tropical Forest: Explore a lush rainforest environment filled with tropical fish, reptiles, and amphibians.

Shark SeaTube: Walk through an underwater tunnel surrounded by a variety of sharks, including sand tiger sharks and nurse sharks.

Ohio Lakes and Rivers: Learn about the aquatic ecosystems of Ohio, including the creatures that inhabit the state's lakes and rivers.

Coastal Boardwalk: Discover creatures from coastal regions, including horseshoe crabs, rays, and seahorses.

Invertebrate Invaders: Get up close with unique and sometimes bizarre marine invertebrates, such as jellyfish and sea stars.

Interactive Touch Tanks: The aquarium offers interactive touch tanks where you can gently touch and interact with marine animals like stingrays and horseshoe crabs. It's a hands-on experience that's especially enjoyable for children.

Educational Programs: The Greater Cleveland Aquarium provides educational programs, talks, and animal feedings throughout the day. These programs offer insights into marine life, conservation efforts, and animal behaviors.

Conservation: The aquarium is committed to conservation and often participates in programs to protect endangered species and promote sustainable practices.

Children's Play Area: The aquarium has a designated children's play area where young visitors can enjoy age-appropriate activities and educational exhibits.

Gift Shop: The on-site gift shop offers a variety of marine-themed merchandise, including souvenirs, books, and toys.

Aquatic-Themed Events: The Greater Cleveland Aquarium occasionally hosts special events, themed nights, and educational workshops. Check the aquarium's website for information on current events and programs.

Accessibility: The aquarium strives to provide accessibility for all visitors, including those with disabilities. Wheelchair-accessible facilities are available.

Hours and Admission: Be sure to check the aquarium's website for current hours of operation, admission fees, and any special exhibitions or events.

Visiting the Greater Cleveland Aquarium is an opportunity to immerse yourself in the underwater world, learn about marine ecosystems, and appreciate the beauty and diversity of aquatic life. Whether you're a marine enthusiast, a family with children, or simply looking for an enjoyable and educational outing, the aquarium offers an engaging and memorable experience for visitors of all ages.

17.Explore the USS Cod Submarine Memorial.

Exploring the USS Cod Submarine Memorial in Cleveland provides a unique opportunity to step back in time and experience a World War II-era submarine. Here's what you can expect when you visit the USS Cod:

Historical Significance: The USS Cod (SS-224) is a Gato-class submarine that served during World War II. It is now a National Historic Landmark and is preserved as a museum ship in Cleveland. The submarine played a crucial role in several Pacific Theater campaigns during the war.

Guided Tours: Visitors to the USS Cod can take guided tours of the submarine led by knowledgeable and passionate tour guides. These tours provide insights into the submarine's history, its crew, and the experiences of submariners during World War II.

Interior Exploration: You'll have the opportunity to explore the interior of the submarine, including the cramped living quarters, control room, mess hall, and torpedo rooms. It's a fascinating look at the tight quarters and conditions that submariners endured during wartime.

Travel to Cleveland Ohio

Authentic Artifacts: The submarine is filled with authentic artifacts, equipment, and displays that offer a glimpse into life on a WWII submarine. You'll see everything from the crew's personal belongings to the intricate machinery used to operate the sub.

Educational Exhibits: The USS Cod features educational exhibits that explain the history and significance of the submarine and its role in naval operations during the war. These exhibits help visitors gain a deeper understanding of the submarine's service.

Historical Information: Throughout the tour, guides provide historical information about the submarine's missions, battles, and accomplishments during WWII.

Photography: You're welcome to take photographs during your visit, making it possible to capture the unique experience of exploring a historic submarine.

Accessibility: The USS Cod strives to provide accessibility for visitors, including those with disabilities. However, keep in mind that the interior of the submarine can be cramped and may pose challenges for some visitors.

Hours and Admission: Check the USS Cod's website for current hours of operation, admission fees, and any special events or programs.

Visiting the USS Cod Submarine Memorial is a remarkable opportunity to pay tribute to the bravery and sacrifice of the submariners who served during World War II. It offers a hands-on and immersive experience that allows you to step into the shoes of those who served aboard this historic vessel. Whether you're a history enthusiast, a military buff, or simply curious about this period in history, the USS Cod provides a unique and educational experience for visitors of all ages.

18. Discover the Lake View Cemetery.

Exploring Lake View Cemetery in Cleveland offers a chance to immerse yourself in a serene and historic final resting place that also serves as a beautiful park and cultural destination. Here's what you can expect when you visit Lake View Cemetery:

Historical Significance: Lake View Cemetery is one of the most prominent and historic cemeteries in Cleveland. Established in 1869, it is the final resting place of many notable individuals, including industrialists, politicians, and cultural figures.

Beautiful Landscapes: The cemetery's grounds are meticulously landscaped and include lush gardens, rolling hills, tranquil ponds, and winding paths. It's a picturesque setting that provides a sense of peace and contemplation.

Notable Burials: Lake View Cemetery is the final resting place of several notable figures, including President James A. Garfield, industrialist John D. Rockefeller, oil magnate Jeptha Wade, and famed architect Charles F. Schweinfurth, among others. Their ornate mausoleums and monuments are a testament to their historical significance.

Garden Cemetery: Lake View Cemetery follows the "garden cemetery" style, where the natural beauty of the landscape is preserved and enhanced with ornamental plantings and architectural features. The result is a peaceful and park-like environment.

James A. Garfield Monument: The James A. Garfield Monument is one of the most iconic landmarks within the cemetery. This massive memorial honors the 20th President of the United States and features a striking tower that visitors can climb for panoramic views of the surrounding area.

Wade Chapel: Wade Chapel is another notable architectural gem within the cemetery. Designed by Louis Comfort Tiffany, it features stunning stained glass windows and is known for its beautiful interior.

Tours and Programs: Lake View Cemetery offers guided tours and educational programs that provide insights into the history, art, and architecture of the cemetery. These tours may focus on specific sections, notable graves, or the history of the cemetery.

Wildlife and Nature: The cemetery is home to various wildlife, including birds and deer. It's also a peaceful place for birdwatching and enjoying the natural surroundings.

Accessibility: The cemetery strives to provide accessibility for visitors, including those with disabilities. Paths and walkways are well-maintained, but some areas may have hilly terrain.

Travel to Cleveland Ohio

Hours and Rules: Be sure to check the cemetery's website for current hours of operation, rules, and any special events or programs.

Visiting Lake View Cemetery is a unique opportunity to explore a historic and culturally significant site while enjoying the tranquility of a beautifully landscaped park. Whether you're interested in history, architecture, or simply seeking a peaceful place for reflection and contemplation, Lake View Cemetery offers a serene and enriching experience for all visitors.

19. Attend the Cleveland International Film Festival.

Attending the Cleveland International Film Festival (CIFF) is a thrilling cinematic experience that allows you to explore a diverse range of films from around the world. Here's what you can expect when you participate in the CIFF:

Film Selection: CIFF typically showcases a wide variety of films, including feature films, documentaries, short films, and animated works. The festival's programming spans genres, cultures, and themes, providing something for every movie enthusiast.

International and Independent Films: As the name suggests, the CIFF specializes in international cinema and often features films that may not be widely distributed in mainstream theaters. This gives you the opportunity to discover hidden gems and unique perspectives.

World Premieres and Debuts: CIFF often hosts world premieres, regional premieres, and debuts of films, including those by emerging filmmakers. It's a chance to be among the first to see groundbreaking works of cinema.

Filmmaker Q&A Sessions: Many screenings are followed by Q&A sessions with directors, producers, actors, and other key figures involved in the films. This offers insight into the creative process and allows for engaging discussions.

Special Screenings: In addition to the regular film screenings, CIFF may host special events and screenings, such as opening night ceremonies, closing night celebrations, and themed film series.

Educational Programs: CIFF offers educational programs and workshops that provide opportunities for aspiring filmmakers and those interested in the industry to learn from experienced professionals.

Audience Engagement: The festival often encourages audience engagement through voting for favorite films, discussions, and forums that foster dialogue about the films and their themes.

Film Categories: Films at CIFF cover a wide array of categories, including drama, comedy, documentary, LGBTQ+ themes, social issues, and more. The festival's program is usually organized into thematic groupings.

Location and Venues: CIFF screenings typically take place at various theaters and venues in and around Cleveland. Be sure to check the festival's website or program for the exact locations and showtimes.

Ticketing and Passes: CIFF offers various ticketing options, including single tickets for specific screenings, ticket packages, and festival passes that provide access to multiple films. Tickets and passes can be purchased in advance.

Accessibility: The festival strives to be accessible to all attendees, including those with disabilities. Venues typically offer wheelchair-accessible seating and facilities.

Dates: CIFF is an annual event with specific dates each year. Be sure to check the festival's official website for the most up-to-date information on dates, schedules, and ticketing.

The Cleveland International Film Festival is a celebration of cinema, culture, and storytelling. Whether you're a film enthusiast, a filmmaker, or simply someone who enjoys a good movie, the festival provides a vibrant and enriching experience that allows you to explore the world through the lens of filmmakers from diverse backgrounds.

20. Take a ride on the Cuyahoga Valley Scenic Railroad.

Taking a ride on the Cuyahoga Valley Scenic Railroad is a delightful way to experience the natural beauty and history of the Cuyahoga Valley National Park

Travel to Cleveland Ohio

and the surrounding area. Here's what you can expect when you embark on a journey with the Cuyahoga Valley Scenic Railroad:

Scenic Beauty: The Cuyahoga Valley Scenic Railroad travels through the picturesque Cuyahoga Valley, offering passengers stunning views of lush forests, rolling hills, the meandering Cuyahoga River, and various wildlife. The changing seasons bring their own unique charm, with vibrant fall foliage, snowy winter landscapes, and blooming spring and summer scenery.

Historical Significance: The railroad has a rich history dating back to the early 20th century. Riding on vintage, well-preserved trains allows you to step back in time and experience a piece of railroad history.

Route Options: The Cuyahoga Valley Scenic Railroad offers various route options, including round-trip excursions and one-way rides. Popular routes include trips from Rockside Station to Akron Northside Station or Peninsula Depot. Each route provides a different perspective of the valley.

Narration: During the journey, knowledgeable narrators often provide commentary about the history, ecology, and cultural significance of the Cuyahoga Valley, making the ride both educational and entertaining.

Special Events: The railroad hosts special events and themed excursions throughout the year. These can include holiday-themed rides, wine and beer tastings, and family-friendly activities. Be sure to check the railroad's schedule for upcoming events.

Accessibility: The Cuyahoga Valley Scenic Railroad strives to be accessible to all passengers, including those with disabilities. Some railcars are equipped with wheelchair-accessible features, and the staff is accommodating.

Food and Beverages: Depending on the route and service class you choose, you may have the option to purchase snacks, beverages, or even full meals on board.

Photography: The scenic landscapes along the route provide ample opportunities for photography. Be sure to bring your camera or smartphone to capture the breathtaking views.

Children's Programs: The railroad often offers family-friendly programs and activities for young passengers, making it an enjoyable experience for families with children.

Ticketing: Tickets for the Cuyahoga Valley Scenic Railroad can be purchased in advance online or at the stations. Depending on the route and class of service, ticket prices may vary.

Seasonal Operations: The railroad operates seasonally, with schedules and routes that may change based on the time of year. Be sure to check the official website for current operating hours and availability.

A ride on the Cuyahoga Valley Scenic Railroad is a memorable and relaxing experience that allows you to connect with nature, explore history, and enjoy the tranquil beauty of the Cuyahoga Valley. Whether you're a nature enthusiast, a history buff, or simply seeking a leisurely outing, the scenic railroad offers a unique perspective of this national park and its surroundings.

21. Explore the West Side Market.

Exploring the West Side Market in Cleveland is a culinary and cultural adventure that allows you to savor a wide variety of fresh and gourmet foods while immersing yourself in a historic market setting. Here's what you can expect when you visit the West Side Market:

Historical Significance: The West Side Market is one of the oldest public markets in the United States, dating back to 1840. Its historic building, with its distinctive clock tower, is an architectural gem and an iconic landmark in Cleveland.

Vibrant Atmosphere: When you step inside the West Side Market, you'll be greeted by a bustling and vibrant atmosphere. The market is a hub of activity, with a diverse crowd of shoppers, food enthusiasts, and tourists.

Food Vendors: The market is home to a wide array of food vendors, including butchers, bakers, fishmongers, cheese shops, spice merchants, delis, and fresh produce stands. You'll find everything from artisanal cheeses and cured meats to freshly baked bread and pastries.

International Flavors: One of the highlights of the West Side Market is its international cuisine offerings. You can sample dishes and ingredients from various cultures, including Italian, Middle Eastern, Polish, Mexican, and more. Don't miss the chance to try a variety of ethnic foods.

Travel to Cleveland Ohio

Fresh and Local: Many of the vendors at the West Side Market pride themselves on offering fresh, locally sourced, and often organic products. It's an excellent place to support local farmers and artisans.

Food Sampling: Vendors often offer samples of their products, allowing you to taste before you buy. This makes for a fun and interactive shopping experience.

Ready-to-Eat Options: In addition to fresh ingredients, the market also features stalls selling ready-to-eat foods. You can enjoy hot meals, sandwiches, and snacks from various culinary traditions.

Craft Beverages: Some vendors offer craft beverages, including coffee, tea, fresh juices, and more, providing a refreshing break during your visit.

Artisanal and Specialty Items: Beyond food, you'll find stalls selling artisanal and specialty products, such as handmade chocolates, spices, kitchen gadgets, and unique culinary finds.

Cultural Diversity: The market reflects the cultural diversity of Cleveland, making it a melting pot of flavors, traditions, and culinary influences.

Shopping and Souvenirs: The West Side Market is not only a place to shop for food but also for souvenirs and gifts. You can find local Cleveland-themed items and market memorabilia.

Events and Workshops: The market occasionally hosts special events, cooking demonstrations, and workshops. Check the market's website for information on upcoming events.

Operating Hours: Be sure to check the market's official website for current operating hours, as they may vary by day of the week and season.

Visiting the West Side Market is a sensory delight, offering an opportunity to explore the rich culinary heritage of Cleveland while soaking in the vibrant market atmosphere. Whether you're a foodie, a lover of fresh ingredients, or simply looking for a unique shopping experience, the West Side Market is a must-visit destination in Cleveland.

22. Attend a Cleveland Orchestra performance at Severance Hall.

Attending a Cleveland Orchestra performance at Severance Hall is a world-class musical experience that allows you to enjoy the exceptional talents of one of the finest orchestras in the world. Here's what you can expect when you attend a performance at Severance Hall:

Historic Venue: Severance Hall is a historic and architecturally stunning concert hall located in Cleveland's University Circle neighborhood. It's renowned for its exceptional acoustics and beautiful design, making it an ideal setting for classical music performances.

Orchestral Excellence: The Cleveland Orchestra is one of the most acclaimed orchestras globally, with a rich history of excellence and a legacy of outstanding performances. Under the direction of renowned conductors, the orchestra presents a wide range of classical and contemporary music.

Diverse Repertoire: The orchestra's repertoire spans classical masterpieces, contemporary compositions, and innovative programming that explores different styles and eras of music. You can expect to hear symphonies, concertos, chamber music, and more.

World-Class Soloists: Cleveland Orchestra performances often feature world-class soloists, including renowned pianists, violinists, cellists, and vocalists. These collaborations add depth and virtuosity to the concerts.

Conductors: The orchestra works with a roster of distinguished conductors, including its music director, to interpret and present a diverse array of musical works.

Special Performances: Throughout the year, Severance Hall hosts special performances, including holiday concerts, educational programs, and collaborations with guest artists and ensembles. These events offer unique and memorable musical experiences.

Cultural Experience: Attending a Cleveland Orchestra performance is not just about the music; it's also an opportunity to immerse yourself in Cleveland's cultural scene. The orchestra contributes to the city's vibrant arts community.

Dress Code: While there is no strict dress code, many attendees choose to dress in semi-formal or formal attire, especially for evening performances. However, feel free to wear what makes you comfortable.

Tickets and Reservations: It's advisable to purchase tickets in advance, especially for popular performances. Tickets can be purchased online through the Cleveland Orchestra's website or by phone. Subscriptions and season tickets are also available.

Pre-Show Dining: Severance Hall offers pre-concert dining options at the restaurant located within the hall. Reservations are recommended if you plan to dine before the performance.

Accessibility: Severance Hall is committed to providing accessibility for all patrons, including those with disabilities. Accessible seating, services, and facilities are available.

Arrival: Plan to arrive at the hall well before the performance starts to allow time for parking and to settle into your seat. Ushers are available to assist with seating and any questions you may have.

Attending a Cleveland Orchestra performance at Severance Hall is a cultural treasure, offering a chance to experience the beauty and power of classical music performed at the highest level. Whether you're a seasoned classical music enthusiast or a newcomer to the genre, the orchestra's concerts are a testament to artistic excellence and are sure to leave a lasting impression.

23. Visit the A Christmas Story House and Museum.

Visiting the A Christmas Story House and Museum in Cleveland is a nostalgic and delightful experience that allows you to step into the world of the classic holiday film "A Christmas Story." Here's what you can expect when you visit this iconic attraction:

Film Nostalgia: The A Christmas Story House and Museum celebrates the beloved 1983 film "A Christmas Story," directed by Bob Clark. The movie has become a cherished part of holiday traditions for many, and this attraction brings the film's scenes to life.

The House: The centerpiece of the experience is the actual house used in the filming of "A Christmas Story." The house has been meticulously restored to resemble the Parker family home, complete with period-accurate furnishings and decor.

Guided Tours: Visitors can take guided tours of the house, led by knowledgeable and enthusiastic guides who share behind-the-scenes stories about the film's production and trivia about the house itself. You'll explore various rooms, including the living room, kitchen, and Ralphie's bedroom.

Photo Opportunities: The house provides numerous photo opportunities, allowing you to recreate iconic scenes from the film. Snap a picture at the famous "leg lamp" window or while sitting in the kitchen, just like in the movie.

Museum: Adjacent to the house, you'll find the A Christmas Story Museum, which houses a vast collection of props, costumes, memorabilia, and original film-related items from "A Christmas Story." It's a treasure trove for fans of the film.

Gift Shop: The gift shop offers a wide range of "A Christmas Story" merchandise, including leg lamps, Red Ryder BB guns, holiday ornaments, and more. It's a great place to find unique holiday gifts and souvenirs.

Events and Activities: The A Christmas Story House and Museum often hosts special events and activities throughout the year, including holiday-themed events, screenings of the film, and appearances by cast members.

Interactive Exhibits: The museum features interactive exhibits that allow you to engage with the film's memorable moments and learn about its production.

Hours and Admission: Be sure to check the attraction's official website for current hours of operation, admission fees, and any special events or programs.

Accessibility: The A Christmas Story House and Museum is committed to providing accessibility for all visitors, including those with disabilities. Be sure to inquire about any specific accommodations you may need.

Parking: There is parking available near the attraction, but it can be limited during peak times, so plan accordingly.

Travel to Cleveland Ohio

Visiting the A Christmas Story House and Museum is a heartwarming journey into the holiday spirit and a chance to relive the magic of a cherished film. Whether you're a fan of "A Christmas Story," seeking a unique holiday experience, or simply looking to capture the nostalgia of Christmastime, this attraction offers a memorable and festive adventure for visitors of all ages.

24. Explore the Cleveland Grays Armory Museum.

Exploring the Cleveland Grays Armory Museum is a fascinating journey through the military history of Cleveland and the United States. Here's what you can expect when you visit this historic museum:

Historical Significance: The Cleveland Grays Armory Museum is located in the historic Grays Armory, which was built in 1893. The armory has a rich history, serving as the headquarters of the Cleveland Grays, a volunteer militia unit established in 1837. It played a role in various military actions and served the community in times of need.

Museum Exhibits: The museum features a diverse collection of military artifacts, uniforms, weapons, and memorabilia spanning from the early 19th century to the present day. Exhibits offer insights into the evolution of military technology, uniforms, and the role of the Cleveland Grays in local and national history.

Historical Displays: Visitors can explore historical displays that highlight the contributions of the Cleveland Grays during the Civil War, the Spanish-American War, and both World Wars. The museum also covers the history of the armory building itself.

Weaponry: The museum showcases an impressive array of historical firearms, from muskets and rifles to handguns. You can learn about the development and use of various weapons throughout history.

Uniforms and Equipment: Military uniforms and equipment from different eras are on display, providing a visual timeline of how military attire has evolved over time.

Educational Programs: The Cleveland Grays Armory Museum offers educational programs and guided tours that delve into the history and significance of the Cleveland Grays and the armory. These programs are ideal for students and history enthusiasts.

Archives: The museum houses an archives collection containing documents, photographs, and records related to the Cleveland Grays and military history. Researchers and historians can access these resources for in-depth study.

Events: The armory often hosts special events, lectures, and reenactments that bring history to life. Check the museum's website or calendar for information on upcoming events.

Accessibility: The Cleveland Grays Armory Museum is committed to providing accessibility for all visitors, including those with disabilities. Be sure to inquire about specific accommodations you may need.

Hours and Admission: Check the museum's official website for current hours of operation, admission fees, and any special exhibitions or events.

Visiting the Cleveland Grays Armory Museum is a chance to step back in time and gain a deeper appreciation for the military history of Cleveland and the role of local militia units. Whether you're a history buff, a student, or simply curious about the legacy of the Cleveland Grays, the museum offers an enriching experience that honors the contributions of those who served.

25. Explore the Crawford Auto-Aviation Museum.

Exploring the Crawford Auto-Aviation Museum in Cleveland offers a captivating journey through the history of automobiles and aviation. Here's what you can expect when you visit this fascinating museum:

Historical Significance: The Crawford Auto-Aviation Museum is part of the Western Reserve Historical Society and is housed in the historic 1917 Hay-McKinney Mansion. The museum showcases the development of transportation in the United States, with a focus on automobiles and aviation.

Impressive Collection: The museum features an extensive and diverse collection of automobiles, aircraft, motorcycles, bicycles, and related artifacts. The

Travel to Cleveland Ohio

collection spans from the late 19th century to the mid-20th century, offering a comprehensive look at the evolution of transportation.

Antique and Vintage Vehicles: Visitors can admire beautifully restored antique and vintage automobiles from various eras. The museum's collection includes classic cars, luxury vehicles, and early prototypes. You'll see vehicles from manufacturers such as Ford, Packard, Duesenberg, and more.

Aviation History: The museum's aviation section showcases aircraft, aircraft engines, and aviation memorabilia. It explores the history of flight, including the early days of aviation, World War I and II aircraft, and innovations in aviation technology.

Interactive Exhibits: Some exhibits in the Crawford Auto-Aviation Museum are interactive, allowing visitors to engage with the history of transportation and learn about the mechanics of vehicles and aircraft.

Historical Context: Throughout the museum, you'll find displays and information that provide historical context, highlighting the social, economic, and technological changes associated with transportation innovations.

Educational Programs: The museum offers educational programs, workshops, and events for all ages, making it an ideal destination for families and students interested in STEM (science, technology, engineering, and mathematics) subjects.

Special Exhibitions: The museum hosts special exhibitions that focus on specific aspects of transportation history, innovations, and related topics. These exhibitions provide fresh perspectives and experiences for returning visitors.

Accessibility: The Crawford Auto-Aviation Museum is committed to providing accessibility for all visitors, including those with disabilities. Be sure to inquire about specific accommodations you may need.

Hours and Admission: Check the museum's official website for current hours of operation, admission fees, and any special exhibitions or events.

Visiting the Crawford Auto-Aviation Museum is a thrilling opportunity to immerse yourself in the history of transportation and innovation. Whether you're a car enthusiast, aviation buff, history lover, or simply looking for an engaging and educational experience, the museum offers a fascinating journey through time and technology, showcasing the evolution of vehicles and flight.

26. Go to the Great Lakes Brewing Company for a brewery tour.

Visiting the Great Lakes Brewing Company in Cleveland for a brewery tour is a delightful experience that allows you to learn about the craft of brewing while enjoying some of the region's finest beers. Here's what you can expect when you take a tour of this iconic brewery:

Historic Brewery: The Great Lakes Brewing Company is located in a historic building in the Ohio City neighborhood of Cleveland. The brewery has a rich history, dating back to 1988, and is known for its commitment to quality, sustainability, and community engagement.

Guided Tours: The brewery offers guided tours that take you behind the scenes of the brewing process. Knowledgeable tour guides lead you through the production area, explaining each step of brewing, from selecting ingredients to fermentation and packaging.

Brewing Process: During the tour, you'll learn about the brewing process, the different styles of beer produced by the brewery, and the unique characteristics of Great Lakes Brewing Company's beers. It's an educational experience for beer enthusiasts and novices alike.

Sustainability: The brewery is dedicated to sustainability practices and often showcases its efforts during the tour. You'll learn about their commitment to environmental responsibility and community involvement.

Historical Insights: The building itself has historical significance, and you'll gain insights into the architecture and history of the brewery's location.

Tasting Room: After the tour, many brewery tours include a visit to the tasting room or brewpub, where you can sample a selection of Great Lakes Brewing Company's beers. It's an opportunity to savor their award-winning brews and find your favorites.

Gift Shop: The brewery often has a gift shop on-site where you can purchase merchandise, including beer-related items, glassware, clothing, and more.

Travel to Cleveland Ohio

Events and Special Releases: Great Lakes Brewing Company hosts events and releases special and seasonal beers throughout the year. Check their website for information on upcoming events and new beer releases.

Reservations: It's a good idea to make reservations for brewery tours, especially during peak times or if you have a large group.

Accessibility: The brewery strives to provide accessibility for all visitors, including those with disabilities. Be sure to inquire about specific accommodations you may need.

Visiting the Great Lakes Brewing Company for a brewery tour is an opportunity to appreciate the art and science of craft brewing while enjoying the company's renowned beers. Whether you're a craft beer aficionado, a history enthusiast, or simply looking for a fun and educational outing, the brewery tour offers an engaging experience for visitors of legal drinking age.

27. Attend the Cleveland International Piano Competition.

Attending the Cleveland International Piano Competition is a remarkable opportunity to witness world-class pianists compete and showcase their extraordinary talents. Here's what you can expect when you attend this prestigious piano competition:

Piano Excellence: The Cleveland International Piano Competition is renowned for attracting some of the most accomplished and promising pianists from around the world. Competitors are selected through a rigorous screening process, ensuring that you'll witness top-tier performances.

Repertoire Variety: The competition features a diverse range of repertoire, spanning classical compositions from various periods, as well as contemporary works. You can expect to hear masterpieces by composers such as Beethoven, Chopin, Mozart, and more.

Solo Performances: During the competition, each pianist typically performs solo pieces, allowing you to appreciate their technical skill, artistry, and interpretation of the music.

Orchestral Collaboration: In the final rounds, finalists often have the opportunity to perform with an orchestra, showcasing their ability to collaborate with other musicians and deliver stunning concerto performances.

World-Renowned Judges: Distinguished judges, often comprised of accomplished pianists and musicians, evaluate the competitors' performances. Their expertise ensures fair and informed assessments.

Seminars and Masterclasses: In addition to the competition itself, the event may include seminars, lectures, and masterclasses featuring renowned pianists and educators. These sessions offer insights into piano technique, interpretation, and musical appreciation.

Prizes and Awards: The competition typically awards prizes and scholarships to outstanding pianists, helping to support and advance their careers in the world of classical music.

Audience Engagement: Audience members play a crucial role in the competition by providing support and applause for the competitors. The excitement and energy of the audience add to the overall experience.

Tickets and Schedule: Be sure to check the competition's official website for information on ticket availability, performance schedules, and any special events associated with the competition.

Venue: The competition is often held at a prestigious concert hall or venue in Cleveland, providing an elegant and acoustically superb setting for the performances.

Accessibility: The organizers strive to provide accessibility for all patrons, including those with disabilities. Be sure to inquire about specific accommodations you may need.

Dates: The Cleveland International Piano Competition is typically held on specific dates, so check the official website for the most up-to-date information on schedules and events.

Attending the Cleveland International Piano Competition is a unique opportunity to immerse yourself in the world of classical music, witness exceptional piano performances, and support emerging and established talents in the field of piano playing. Whether you're a seasoned classical music aficionado

Travel to Cleveland Ohio

or simply seeking an enriching cultural experience, this competition offers a captivating and memorable musical journey.

28.Explore the Children's Museum of Cleveland.

Exploring the Children's Museum of Cleveland offers an engaging and interactive experience for children and families. Here's what you can expect when you visit this dynamic museum:

Hands-On Learning: The Children's Museum of Cleveland is designed with interactive exhibits and activities that encourage hands-on learning and exploration. Children have the opportunity to engage with exhibits in a fun and educational way.

Imagination and Creativity: The museum's exhibits are often centered around themes that spark imagination and creativity. From pretend play areas to art and science activities, children can unleash their creativity and curiosity.

Age-Appropriate Zones: The museum is divided into age-appropriate zones to cater to various developmental stages. There are areas designed for infants, toddlers, preschoolers, and older children, ensuring that each child's needs and interests are addressed.

Art and Expression: Art-focused exhibits and activities allow children to express themselves through painting, drawing, sculpture, and other creative outlets. Artistic exploration is encouraged.

Science and Exploration: Science-themed exhibits promote discovery and understanding of the natural world. Children can experiment, solve puzzles, and engage in hands-on science activities.

Cultural Experiences: Some exhibits may offer cultural experiences, introducing children to different traditions, customs, and global perspectives.

Outdoor Play: Depending on the museum's facilities, there may be outdoor play areas or gardens where children can enjoy fresh air and physical activity.

Special Programs: The Children's Museum of Cleveland often hosts special programs, workshops, and events throughout the year. These programs may align with holidays, seasons, or educational themes.

Birthday Parties: The museum may offer birthday party packages, providing a unique and fun setting for children's celebrations.

Gift Shop: A museum gift shop may offer educational toys, books, and souvenirs related to the exhibits, allowing families to extend the learning experience at home.

Accessibility: The museum is designed to be accessible to all visitors, including those with disabilities. Be sure to inquire about specific accommodations you may need.

Hours and Admission: Check the museum's official website for current hours of operation, admission fees, membership options, and any special exhibitions or events.

Visiting the Children's Museum of Cleveland provides a wonderful opportunity for families to bond, play, and learn together. It fosters a love of learning, exploration, and creativity in children while offering a fun and educational experience for all. Whether you're a parent, grandparent, or caregiver, the museum offers a welcoming and enriching environment for children to thrive.

29. Go fishing on Lake Erie.

Fishing on Lake Erie is a popular and rewarding outdoor activity, known for its abundant fish populations and scenic beauty. Here's what you can expect when you go fishing on Lake Erie:

Diverse Fish Species: Lake Erie is home to a wide variety of fish species, making it a prime destination for anglers. Some of the most sought-after catches include walleye, perch, smallmouth bass, largemouth bass, steelhead trout, and catfish.

Fishing Charters: Many anglers choose to go on guided fishing charters when fishing on Lake Erie. Charter boats are equipped with experienced captains who know the best fishing spots and techniques. They provide all the necessary equipment and can accommodate both novice and experienced anglers.

Travel to Cleveland Ohio

Scenic Beauty: Lake Erie offers stunning views and a peaceful atmosphere for fishing. Whether you're fishing from a boat or the shoreline, you'll have the opportunity to enjoy the lake's clear waters and picturesque surroundings.

Seasonal Variations: Fishing on Lake Erie can be enjoyed year-round, but the best times for certain species vary. Spring and summer are prime for walleye and perch, while fall brings steelhead trout runs. Ice fishing is popular in the winter months.

Fishing Tournaments: Lake Erie hosts numerous fishing tournaments throughout the year, attracting anglers from across the region. These events offer competitive opportunities and often come with cash prizes.

Licensing and Regulations: Before you go fishing on Lake Erie, be sure to obtain the necessary fishing license and check for any fishing regulations and size limits that may apply to specific species. Regulations are in place to protect the fish populations and the ecosystem.

Boat Rentals: If you have boating experience, you can rent boats to explore the lake on your own. Some marinas offer boat rentals, but be sure to inquire about availability and safety guidelines.

Bait and Tackle Shops: There are bait and tackle shops in the Lake Erie region where you can purchase fishing gear, bait, and supplies. Local experts can provide advice on the best bait to use for specific fish species.

Fish Cleaning Services: Some marinas and fishing charters offer fish cleaning services, allowing you to take your catch home ready to cook.

Safety Precautions: Safety should be a priority when fishing on Lake Erie. Be sure to wear appropriate clothing, sunscreen, and life jackets if you're on a boat. Stay hydrated and be aware of weather conditions and water currents.

Conservation: Responsible fishing practices are essential to protect the lake's ecosystem. Be sure to dispose of trash properly and follow catch-and-release guidelines for certain species when necessary.

Fishing on Lake Erie provides a memorable outdoor experience, whether you're a seasoned angler or a beginner. With its diverse fish populations and natural beauty, Lake Erie offers a rewarding and relaxing environment for enjoying the sport of fishing.

30. Take a yoga class at the Cleveland Yoga Studio.

Taking a yoga class at the Cleveland Yoga Studio is an opportunity to rejuvenate your mind and body through the practice of yoga. Here's what you can expect when you attend a class at this studio:

Diverse Classes: Cleveland Yoga Studio typically offers a wide range of yoga classes suitable for all levels, from beginners to advanced practitioners. Classes may include Hatha, Vinyasa, Power Yoga, Yin Yoga, Restorative Yoga, and more.

Experienced Instructors: The studio is staffed by experienced and certified yoga instructors who are dedicated to helping students deepen their practice. Instructors often provide guidance on alignment, breath control, and mindfulness.

Welcoming Environment: The studio aims to create a welcoming and inclusive environment where students of all backgrounds and abilities can practice yoga comfortably. It's a place to connect with like-minded individuals and build a sense of community.

Physical and Mental Benefits: Yoga offers a wide range of physical and mental benefits, including improved flexibility, strength, balance, and relaxation. Many practitioners find that yoga helps reduce stress, enhance mindfulness, and promote overall well-being.

Class Variety: In addition to traditional yoga classes, the studio may offer specialized workshops, events, and teacher training programs. These offerings allow students to deepen their knowledge and explore different aspects of yoga.

Equipment: The studio typically provides yoga mats and props, but you're welcome to bring your own if you prefer. Comfortable clothing that allows for movement is recommended.

Class Length: Classes can vary in length, with options for quick 60-minute sessions or longer, more immersive experiences.

Travel to Cleveland Ohio

Class Levels: Classes are often categorized by levels such as beginner, intermediate, and advanced, allowing you to choose the level that suits your practice.

Class Schedules: Check the studio's official website or contact them directly for current class schedules, descriptions, and registration information.

Membership and Pricing: The studio may offer various membership packages or drop-in rates. Be sure to inquire about pricing options and any introductory offers for new students.

Online Classes: Some studios offer virtual or online classes, allowing you to practice yoga from the comfort of your own home if you prefer.

Accessibility: The studio typically strives to be accessible to all students, including those with physical limitations. Inquire about any accommodations or modifications that may be available.

Yoga is a transformative practice that can enhance your physical and mental well-being. Whether you're seeking relaxation, stress relief, improved flexibility, or a way to connect with your inner self, attending a yoga class at the Cleveland Yoga Studio offers a supportive and nurturing environment to explore the benefits of yoga.

31. Visit the International Women's Air and Space Museum.

Visiting the International Women's Air and Space Museum in Cleveland is an inspiring journey through the history of women's contributions to aviation and space exploration. Here's what you can expect when you visit this remarkable museum:

Celebrating Women in Aviation: The International Women's Air and Space Museum (IWASM) is dedicated to preserving and showcasing the achievements of women in aviation and aerospace. It highlights the stories of pioneering female aviators, astronauts, engineers, and other professionals who have made significant contributions to the industry.

Exhibits and Artifacts: The museum features a diverse collection of exhibits and artifacts, including aircraft models, photographs, memorabilia, and personal items that belonged to prominent women in aviation and space. These exhibits provide insights into their lives, careers, and groundbreaking achievements.

Interactive Displays: Some exhibits may include interactive displays, allowing visitors to engage with the history of aviation and aerospace in an educational and hands-on way.

Inspiring Stories: As you explore the museum, you'll encounter stories of trailblazing women who shattered gender barriers and paved the way for future generations of female aviators and astronauts. These stories serve as a source of inspiration for all visitors.

Educational Programs: The IWASM often hosts educational programs, lectures, and events that promote awareness of the role of women in aviation and space exploration. These programs offer opportunities to learn from experts and connect with fellow aviation enthusiasts.

Women of Achievement Hall: The museum's Women of Achievement Hall honors notable women who have made significant contributions to aviation and aerospace. It's a place to pay tribute to their legacies and contributions.

Gift Shop: The museum typically has a gift shop where you can purchase aviation-themed merchandise, books, and souvenirs related to women in aviation and space.

Accessibility: The IWASM is committed to providing accessibility for all visitors, including those with disabilities. Be sure to inquire about specific accommodations you may need.

Hours and Admission: Check the museum's official website for current hours of operation, admission fees, and any special exhibitions or events.

Visiting the International Women's Air and Space Museum offers a chance to celebrate the achievements of remarkable women who have played pivotal roles in the history of aviation and space exploration. Whether you have a passion for aviation, an interest in history, or simply want to learn about the incredible contributions of women in these fields, the museum provides a unique and inspiring experience for all ages.

32. Explore the Cleveland Police Museum.

Exploring the Cleveland Police Museum offers a glimpse into the history of law enforcement in Cleveland and the dedicated men and women who serve the community. Here's what you can expect when you visit this unique museum:

Historical Significance: The Cleveland Police Museum is dedicated to preserving the history of the Cleveland Division of Police, which has served the city since its establishment in the 19th century. The museum highlights the evolution of policing in Cleveland.

Exhibits and Artifacts: The museum features a diverse collection of exhibits and artifacts related to law enforcement, including police uniforms, badges, equipment, vehicles, and memorabilia. These items provide insights into the daily lives and duties of police officers throughout the years.

Historical Cases: Some exhibits may focus on notable historical cases and investigations conducted by the Cleveland police. These displays shed light on the challenges faced by law enforcement and the efforts to maintain public safety.

Community Engagement: The museum often emphasizes the importance of community engagement and collaboration between law enforcement and the public. It may showcase programs and initiatives aimed at building trust and positive relationships between the police and the community.

K-9 Unit: Many police museums feature exhibits dedicated to K-9 units and police dogs. These displays highlight the critical role that police dogs play in law enforcement operations.

Educational Programs: The Cleveland Police Museum may offer educational programs, workshops, and events for visitors of all ages. These programs can provide valuable insights into law enforcement practices and community safety.

Interactive Displays: Some exhibits may include interactive displays that allow visitors to engage with the history of policing and learn about police procedures and tactics.

Historical Context: Throughout the museum, you'll find historical context that helps visitors understand the challenges and changes that have shaped the Cleveland Division of Police over the years.

Gift Shop: The museum often has a gift shop where you can purchase police-themed merchandise, books, and souvenirs related to law enforcement.

Accessibility: The museum strives to provide accessibility for all visitors, including those with disabilities. Be sure to inquire about specific accommodations you may need.

Hours and Admission: Check the museum's official website for current hours of operation, admission fees, and any special exhibitions or events.

Visiting the Cleveland Police Museum is an opportunity to gain a deeper appreciation for the history of law enforcement in the city, as well as the dedication and sacrifices of police officers. Whether you have an interest in law enforcement, local history, or community safety, the museum offers an educational and enlightening experience for visitors of all backgrounds.

33. Attend the Cleveland Asian Festival.

Attending the Cleveland Asian Festival is a vibrant and cultural experience that celebrates the rich diversity and heritage of Asian communities in the Cleveland area. Here's what you can expect when you participate in this lively festival:

Cultural Showcases: The Cleveland Asian Festival typically features a wide range of cultural showcases, including traditional dance performances, music concerts, martial arts demonstrations, and more. These performances highlight the cultural diversity of Asian communities and provide a glimpse into their traditions and artistic expressions.

Food and Cuisine: One of the highlights of the festival is the diverse array of Asian cuisine available. You can savor a wide variety of Asian dishes, from Chinese and Japanese to Korean, Vietnamese, Thai, and more. It's an excellent opportunity to indulge in authentic flavors and culinary delights.

Art and Crafts: The festival often includes art and craft exhibits, where you can explore and purchase traditional and contemporary Asian art, jewelry, clothing, and handcrafted items. It's a great place to find unique gifts and souvenirs.

Interactive Activities: Many Asian festivals offer interactive activities for attendees of all ages. You may have the chance to participate in cultural

Travel to Cleveland Ohio

workshops, learn traditional crafts, or try your hand at Asian calligraphy or origami.

Cultural Displays: The festival typically features cultural displays and exhibitions that showcase the history, traditions, and contributions of Asian communities in the region. These displays can provide valuable insights into the diverse cultures represented.

Vendor Booths: The festival grounds are often filled with vendor booths where local businesses and organizations showcase their products, services, and community initiatives. It's an opportunity to learn about and support Asian-owned businesses.

Community Engagement: Asian festivals often promote community engagement and awareness of social and cultural issues. You may find information booths, discussions, and forums addressing important topics relevant to Asian communities.

Children's Activities: Many Asian festivals offer children's activities and entertainment, making it a family-friendly event. Kids can enjoy games, face painting, storytelling, and more.

Traditional Attire: Attendees and performers often wear traditional clothing representing various Asian cultures, adding to the festive and colorful atmosphere.

Live Entertainment: Live music performances, including traditional and contemporary Asian music, are a common feature of Asian festivals. These performances offer a blend of cultural and modern musical experiences.

Community Unity: The festival serves as a platform for building bridges of understanding and unity among different Asian communities and with the broader community. It's an opportunity to celebrate diversity and foster cultural appreciation.

Accessibility: Event organizers typically strive to provide accessibility for all festivalgoers, including those with disabilities. Be sure to inquire about specific accommodations you may need.

Attending the Cleveland Asian Festival is a chance to immerse yourself in the rich tapestry of Asian cultures, sample delicious cuisine, enjoy vibrant performances, and connect with the local Asian community. It's a celebration of diversity, heritage, and the spirit of unity and inclusion.

34. Take a tour of the James A. Garfield National Historic Site.

Taking a tour of the James A. Garfield National Historic Site provides a fascinating glimpse into the life and times of the 20th President of the United States, James A. Garfield. Here's what you can expect when you visit this historic site:

Historic Residence: The James A. Garfield National Historic Site is centered around the former residence of President Garfield, known as "Lawnfield." This beautifully restored Victorian home offers a step back in time to the late 1800s and provides insights into the daily life of the Garfield family.

Guided Tours: Visitors typically take guided tours of the Lawnfield house, led by knowledgeable park rangers or docents. These tours cover the history of James A. Garfield's life, his political career, and his tragic assassination.

Furnishings and Artifacts: The interior of the house is furnished with period-appropriate items and personal belongings of the Garfield family, offering a glimpse into their lifestyle and tastes.

Historical Significance: The site highlights the significant contributions of President Garfield during his brief presidency, including his advocacy for civil rights and education. It also delves into the circumstances surrounding his assassination and the impact it had on the nation.

Museum Exhibits: The visitor center often features museum exhibits related to Garfield's life, presidency, and the era in which he lived. These exhibits provide additional context and historical information.

Grounds and Gardens: In addition to the house, the site includes beautifully landscaped gardens and grounds where visitors can explore and enjoy the serene surroundings.

Travel to Cleveland Ohio

Visitor Center: The visitor center typically offers information, exhibits, and a gift shop where you can purchase books, souvenirs, and historical items related to President Garfield and the site.

Educational Programs: The James A. Garfield National Historic Site often hosts educational programs, lectures, and special events related to American history and the Garfield presidency.

Accessibility: The site is designed to be accessible to all visitors, including those with disabilities. Be sure to inquire about specific accommodations you may need.

Hours and Admission: Check the site's official website for current hours of operation, admission fees, and any special events or programs.

Visiting the James A. Garfield National Historic Site is an opportunity to gain a deeper understanding of American history and the life and legacy of a remarkable president. Whether you have a passion for history, politics, or simply enjoy exploring historic homes, this site offers a rich and educational experience for visitors of all ages.

35. Explore the Dittrick Medical History Center.

Exploring the Dittrick Medical History Center in Cleveland offers a unique journey through the history of medicine and healthcare. Here's what you can expect when you visit this fascinating center:

Historical Significance: The Dittrick Medical History Center is dedicated to preserving and showcasing the history of medicine, medical innovations, and the development of healthcare practices. It is part of the Dittrick Museum of Medical History, which is affiliated with Case Western Reserve University.

Exhibits and Collections: The center features a diverse collection of medical artifacts, instruments, documents, and rare books that span centuries of medical history. Exhibits cover a wide range of topics, from the evolution of surgical techniques to the history of medical education.

Medical Instruments: You'll have the opportunity to see historical medical instruments and devices, many of which are no longer in use. These items offer insights into the evolution of medical technology and procedures.

Rare Books: The Dittrick Medical History Center houses an extensive collection of rare medical books and manuscripts. These documents provide a window into the scientific and medical knowledge of past eras.

Medical Education: Exhibits often delve into the history of medical education, including the training of physicians and the development of medical schools. You can learn about the challenges and advancements in medical training.

Interactive Displays: Some exhibits may include interactive displays and multimedia presentations that enhance the learning experience. These displays can make the history of medicine come alive.

Historical Context: Throughout the center, you'll find historical context that helps you understand the societal and scientific developments that shaped the practice of medicine over time.

Educational Programs: The Dittrick Medical History Center often hosts educational programs, lectures, and events related to medical history and healthcare. These programs provide opportunities for learning and engagement.

Archival Resources: The center may offer access to archival materials and resources for researchers, scholars, and students interested in medical history and related fields.

Accessibility: The Dittrick Medical History Center is committed to providing accessibility for all visitors, including those with disabilities. Be sure to inquire about specific accommodations you may need.

Hours and Admission: Check the center's official website for current hours of operation, admission fees, and any special exhibitions or events.

Visiting the Dittrick Medical History Center is a chance to gain a deeper appreciation for the evolution of medicine, healthcare practices, and the contributions of medical professionals throughout history. Whether you have a background in healthcare, an interest in scientific history, or simply a curiosity about how medical practices have evolved, this center offers a thought-provoking and educational experience.

Travel to Cleveland Ohio

36. Attend the Cleveland Garlic Festival.

Attending the Cleveland Garlic Festival is a flavorful and aromatic experience that celebrates all things garlic and offers a culinary adventure. Here's what you can expect when you participate in this delicious festival:

Garlic-Inspired Cuisine: The Cleveland Garlic Festival is known for its diverse and creative garlic-infused dishes. You can indulge in a wide range of culinary delights, from garlic-infused appetizers and entrees to garlic ice cream and garlic-themed desserts. It's a paradise for garlic lovers.

Cooking Demonstrations: The festival often features cooking demonstrations and culinary workshops conducted by renowned chefs and culinary experts. These sessions provide insights into cooking with garlic and offer tips and techniques for creating delicious garlic-based dishes at home.

Food Vendors: You'll find numerous food vendors and booths offering a variety of garlic-centric dishes and snacks. It's an opportunity to explore different cuisines and flavors, all with a garlic twist.

Farmers Market: The festival typically includes a farmers market where you can purchase fresh, locally grown garlic and other produce. You can also find artisanal products, spices, and garlic-themed gifts.

Live Music and Entertainment: Many food festivals, including the Cleveland Garlic Festival, feature live music performances, entertainment acts, and cultural displays. It's a lively and enjoyable atmosphere.

Garlic Cooking Competitions: Some festivals host garlic cooking competitions, where chefs or home cooks can showcase their culinary skills by creating unique garlic recipes. These competitions can be both entertaining and educational.

Family-Friendly Activities: The festival often offers family-friendly activities and games, making it an enjoyable outing for all ages. You may find activities such as face painting, garlic-themed arts and crafts, and more.

Beer and Wine Tastings: Some festivals include beer and wine tastings, allowing you to pair garlic dishes with complementary beverages. It's an opportunity to discover new flavors and pairings.

Garlic-Related Merchandise: Vendors at the festival typically offer garlic-related merchandise, including garlic bulbs, garlic presses, cookbooks, and other culinary gadgets.

Accessibility: Event organizers strive to provide accessibility for all festivalgoers, including those with disabilities. Be sure to inquire about specific accommodations you may need.

Dates and Location: Check the festival's official website or local event listings for information on the event's dates, location, admission fees, and any additional details.

Attending the Cleveland Garlic Festival is a sensory delight that allows you to explore the versatility and deliciousness of garlic in various culinary creations. Whether you're a seasoned foodie or simply looking for a fun and flavorful outing, this festival offers a pungent and delectable experience for your taste buds.

37. Go birdwatching at the Lake Erie Nature & Science Center.

Birdwatching at the Lake Erie Nature & Science Center is a wonderful way to connect with nature and observe the diverse bird species that inhabit the area. Here's what you can expect when you visit this natural sanctuary:

Bird Diversity: The Lake Erie Nature & Science Center is situated in an area rich in birdlife, especially during migratory seasons. You can expect to see a variety of bird species, including songbirds, waterfowl, raptors, and more. The center's location near Lake Erie provides an ideal habitat for both resident and migratory birds.

Bird Blind and Observation Areas: Many nature centers, including this one, offer bird blinds or designated observation areas where you can quietly watch birds without disturbing them. These areas are often equipped with binoculars, spotting scopes, and informational signage to enhance your birdwatching experience.

Educational Programs: The Lake Erie Nature & Science Center typically hosts educational programs and guided birdwatching tours led by experienced

Travel to Cleveland Ohio

naturalists. These programs can provide valuable insights into bird behavior, migration patterns, and identification techniques.

Nature Trails: The center may have nature trails or walking paths that wind through different habitats, allowing you to explore diverse ecosystems and spot birds along the way. These trails are often well-maintained and offer opportunities for both novice and experienced birdwatchers.

Bird Identification Resources: Many nature centers provide field guides and reference materials to help you identify the birds you encounter. You can also inquire with staff or volunteers for assistance with bird identification.

Birding Events: Check the center's official website or event calendar for information on birding events, workshops, and special programs that may be offered throughout the year. These events can be a great way to learn more about local birds and connect with fellow birdwatchers.

Photography Opportunities: Birdwatching often presents excellent opportunities for bird photography. Be sure to bring your camera or smartphone to capture the beauty of the birds you encounter.

Family-Friendly Activities: Nature centers often offer family-friendly activities related to birdwatching, making it an educational and enjoyable experience for children and adults alike.

Accessibility: The Lake Erie Nature & Science Center typically strives to provide accessibility for all visitors, including those with disabilities. Be sure to inquire about specific accommodations you may need.

Hours and Admission: Check the center's official website for current hours of operation, admission fees (if any), and any special events or programs related to birdwatching.

Birdwatching at the Lake Erie Nature & Science Center offers a peaceful and immersive outdoor experience, allowing you to connect with the natural world and appreciate the beauty and diversity of birds. Whether you're a seasoned birder or a novice, the center provides a welcoming environment for birdwatching enthusiasts of all levels.

38. Visit the Maltz Museum of Jewish Heritage.

Visiting the Maltz Museum of Jewish Heritage in Cleveland is an opportunity to explore the rich history, culture, and contributions of the Jewish community. Here's what you can expect when you visit this museum:

Celebrating Jewish Heritage: The Maltz Museum is dedicated to preserving and celebrating Jewish heritage and culture. It showcases the history, traditions, and achievements of the Jewish community, both locally and globally.

Exhibits and Artifacts: The museum features a diverse collection of exhibits and artifacts that cover a wide range of topics, from the Holocaust and Jewish immigration to Jewish contributions in various fields, including arts, science, and social justice.

Holocaust and Remembrance: Some exhibits are dedicated to the Holocaust, offering a somber but essential opportunity to learn about this tragic chapter in history. These exhibits often focus on stories of survivors, resistance, and the importance of remembrance.

Interactive Displays: The Maltz Museum may include interactive displays and multimedia presentations that engage visitors and enhance the learning experience. These exhibits can provide a deeper understanding of the subject matter.

Art and Culture: The museum often showcases Jewish art, literature, music, and cultural expressions. You can explore the creativity and artistic contributions of the Jewish community.

Educational Programs: The Maltz Museum typically hosts educational programs, lectures, workshops, and special events related to Jewish history, culture, and social justice. These programs offer opportunities for learning and engagement.

Community Engagement: The museum may highlight the importance of community engagement and social justice initiatives, encouraging visitors to explore themes of tolerance, diversity, and empathy.

Travel to Cleveland Ohio

Children's Activities: Many museums offer family-friendly activities and interactive exhibits for children, making it an educational and enjoyable experience for young visitors.

Gift Shop: The museum often has a gift shop where you can purchase books, Judaica, jewelry, and other items related to Jewish heritage and culture.

Accessibility: The Maltz Museum strives to provide accessibility for all visitors, including those with disabilities. Be sure to inquire about specific accommodations you may need.

Hours and Admission: Check the museum's official website for current hours of operation, admission fees, membership options, and any special exhibitions or events.

Visiting the Maltz Museum of Jewish Heritage offers a chance to learn about the history and contributions of the Jewish community, as well as the broader themes of tolerance, diversity, and social justice. Whether you have a personal interest in Jewish heritage, history, or cultural understanding, this museum provides an educational and enriching experience for visitors of all backgrounds and ages.

39. Attend the Cleveland Comedy Festival.

Attending the Cleveland Comedy Festival promises an evening filled with laughter and entertainment, showcasing talented comedians and providing a fun and lighthearted atmosphere. Here's what you can expect when you participate in this comedy festival:

Stand-Up Comedy: The Cleveland Comedy Festival typically features a lineup of both local and nationally recognized comedians. You can expect a diverse range of stand-up comedy performances that cater to various comedic styles and preferences.

Comedy Competitions: Some comedy festivals include competitions where comedians compete for prizes or recognition. These competitions often bring out the best in comedic talent and provide an opportunity for emerging comedians to shine.

Headliners and Headlining Shows: Many comedy festivals host headlining comedians who are well-known in the industry. These headlining shows often serve as the festival's highlights and feature extended sets by established comedians.

Multiple Venues: Comedy festivals may take place at multiple venues throughout the city. This allows attendees to explore different comedy clubs, theaters, or performance spaces and experience a variety of comedic atmospheres.

Open Mic Nights: Some festivals include open mic nights, where aspiring comedians can showcase their talents. Open mics are often a platform for emerging comedians to test their material and gain exposure.

Special Events: In addition to stand-up performances, comedy festivals may offer special events, such as improv shows, sketch comedy performances, and workshops for those interested in comedy writing and performance.

Audience Interaction: Comedy shows often involve audience interaction, so be prepared for some light-hearted banter with the comedians. Audience participation can add an element of unpredictability to the performances.

Food and Drink: Many comedy venues offer food and drink options, allowing you to enjoy a meal or a beverage while watching the comedy performances.

Laughter and Entertainment: The primary goal of the Cleveland Comedy Festival is to provide laughter and entertainment. It's a chance to relax, enjoy humorous anecdotes, and forget your worries for a while.

Ticketing: Tickets for comedy festival events can vary in price and availability. It's advisable to check the festival's official website or contact the event organizers for information on ticketing options, show schedules, and any age restrictions.

Accessibility: Event organizers typically strive to provide accessibility for all festivalgoers, including those with disabilities. Be sure to inquire about specific accommodations you may need.

Dates and Location: Check the festival's official website or local event listings for information on the event's dates, location, and any additional details.

Attending the Cleveland Comedy Festival is a great way to enjoy a night of laughter, connect with friends or fellow comedy enthusiasts, and appreciate the

Travel to Cleveland Ohio

comedic talents of both emerging and established comedians. It's an experience that brings joy and humor to the forefront, creating lasting memories and moments of pure entertainment.

40.Explore the Ukrainian Museum-Archives.

Exploring the Ukrainian Museum-Archives in Cleveland is an opportunity to immerse yourself in the rich cultural heritage and history of the Ukrainian community. Here's what you can expect when you visit this museum:

Celebrating Ukrainian Culture: The Ukrainian Museum-Archives is dedicated to preserving and showcasing the culture, art, history, and contributions of the Ukrainian people. It serves as a cultural center and a repository of Ukrainian heritage.

Exhibits and Artifacts: The museum features a diverse collection of exhibits and artifacts that cover a wide range of topics related to Ukrainian culture. These exhibits may include traditional Ukrainian clothing, folk art, religious icons, historical documents, and more.

Art and Folklore: Visitors can explore Ukrainian art and folklore through exhibits that highlight traditional crafts, embroidery, pottery, and artistic expressions. These displays provide insights into the creativity and traditions of the Ukrainian community.

Historical Documents: The museum often houses a valuable collection of historical documents, photographs, and archives that shed light on the history of Ukrainian immigrants in the United States, their experiences, and their contributions.

Educational Programs: The Ukrainian Museum-Archives may offer educational programs, lectures, workshops, and cultural events related to Ukrainian heritage. These programs provide opportunities for learning and engagement.

Cultural Events: Check the museum's calendar for cultural events and celebrations, including Ukrainian festivals, music performances, dance presentations, and more. These events often offer a vibrant and festive atmosphere.

People Who Know Publishing

Gift Shop: The museum typically has a gift shop where you can purchase Ukrainian-themed merchandise, books, traditional crafts, and souvenirs.

Accessibility: The Ukrainian Museum-Archives strives to provide accessibility for all visitors, including those with disabilities. Be sure to inquire about specific accommodations you may need.

Hours and Admission: Check the museum's official website for current hours of operation, admission fees, membership options, and any special exhibitions or events.

Visiting the Ukrainian Museum-Archives is an opportunity to appreciate the beauty, traditions, and history of Ukrainian culture. Whether you have a personal connection to Ukraine, an interest in cultural diversity, or a curiosity about the contributions of Ukrainian immigrants to the United States, this museum offers an educational and enriching experience for visitors of all backgrounds and ages.

41. Go ice skating at the Cleveland Foundation Skating Rink.

Ice skating at the Cleveland Foundation Skating Rink is a delightful winter activity that combines fun and exercise in a scenic urban setting. Here's what you can expect when you visit this ice skating rink:

Seasonal Operation: The Cleveland Foundation Skating Rink is typically open during the winter months, from November to February. However, it's a good idea to check the official website or contact the rink for the most up-to-date information on operating hours and seasonal schedules.

Outdoor Ice Skating: The rink is located outdoors, allowing you to enjoy the crisp winter air while gliding across the ice. Skating outdoors in a city setting can be a unique and picturesque experience, especially when surrounded by the city's architecture and skyline.

Skate Rentals: If you don't have your own ice skates, don't worry. Most ice rinks, including this one, offer skate rentals in various sizes. This makes ice skating accessible to individuals and families, even if you're not equipped with your own gear.

Travel to Cleveland Ohio

Family-Friendly: Ice skating is a family-friendly activity, and the Cleveland Foundation Skating Rink welcomes skaters of all ages and skill levels. It's a great way to spend quality time with loved ones during the winter season.

Group Outings: The rink is often a popular destination for group outings, school trips, and corporate events. You can inquire about group rates and reservations if you plan to visit with a large group.

Concessions: Many ice skating rinks have on-site concessions or a nearby snack bar where you can warm up with hot cocoa, enjoy a snack, or refuel with a meal.

Music and Atmosphere: Ice rinks often play music over loudspeakers to enhance the skating experience. The atmosphere is typically festive, especially if you visit during the holiday season.

Skating Lessons: Some ice rinks offer skating lessons for beginners or those looking to improve their skills. If you're new to ice skating, inquire about lesson options.

Events and Theme Nights: The rink may host special events, theme nights, and promotions throughout the season. Keep an eye out for themed skate nights or holiday-related events.

Accessibility: Ice rinks typically provide accessibility for all visitors, including those with disabilities. Inquire about specific accommodations you may need.

Hours and Admission: Check the rink's official website or contact them directly for current hours of operation, admission fees, skate rental prices, and any special events or promotions.

Ice skating at the Cleveland Foundation Skating Rink offers a fun and active way to embrace the winter season, enjoy the outdoors, and create lasting memories with friends and family. Whether you're an experienced skater or stepping onto the ice for the first time, it's an enjoyable winter activity in the heart of the city.

42. Visit the NASA Glenn Research Center.

Visiting the NASA Glenn Research Center in Cleveland provides a unique opportunity to explore the world of space exploration, research, and technology. Here's what you can expect when you visit this renowned NASA facility:

NASA Research and Innovation: The NASA Glenn Research Center is at the forefront of aerospace research, innovation, and technology development. It plays a crucial role in advancing space exploration, aeronautics, and scientific research.

Visitor Center: The Glenn Research Center typically has a visitor center where you can learn about NASA's missions, projects, and contributions to space science and technology. The visitor center often features informative exhibits, displays, and interactive demonstrations.

Educational Programs: The center may offer educational programs, workshops, and presentations aimed at students, educators, and the general public. These programs can provide insights into NASA's work and inspire the next generation of scientists and engineers.

Astronaut Experiences: Depending on the timing of your visit, you may have the opportunity to meet astronauts, attend astronaut presentations, or learn about the experiences of those who have traveled to space.

Spacecraft and Hardware: The visitor center often showcases spacecraft models, hardware, and prototypes used in NASA missions. You can get up close to space-related technology and learn how these components are designed and tested.

Simulators and Interactive Exhibits: Some visitor centers include simulators and interactive exhibits that allow you to experience aspects of space travel, such as simulated launches or spacewalks.

Tours: The NASA Glenn Research Center may offer guided tours of its facilities, giving you a behind-the-scenes look at research labs, test facilities, and engineering workspaces. These tours offer a deeper understanding of NASA's operations.

Lectures and Presentations: Keep an eye out for lectures and presentations by NASA scientists, engineers, and experts. These talks often delve into specific space-related topics and missions.

Gift Shop: The visitor center typically has a gift shop where you can purchase NASA-themed merchandise, space-related books, and souvenirs.

Accessibility: NASA centers strive to provide accessibility for all visitors, including those with disabilities. Be sure to inquire about specific accommodations you may need.

Hours and Admission: Check the NASA Glenn Research Center's official website or contact them directly for current hours of operation, admission fees (if any), and any special events or programs.

Visiting the NASA Glenn Research Center is a chance to get a closer look at the groundbreaking work being done in the field of aerospace research and technology. Whether you have a passion for space exploration, aeronautics, or simply a curiosity about the mysteries of the universe, this NASA facility offers an educational and inspiring experience for visitors of all ages.

43. Explore the Dunham Tavern Museum.

Exploring the Dunham Tavern Museum in Cleveland provides a glimpse into the history of the region and offers insights into early American life. Here's what you can expect when you visit this historic museum:

Historic Site: The Dunham Tavern Museum is situated on the site of one of Cleveland's oldest buildings, Dunham Tavern. This historic structure has been preserved and transformed into a museum to showcase its significance and the history of the area.

Early American History: The museum focuses on the early history of Cleveland and the Western Reserve region of Ohio. You can learn about the pioneers and settlers who played a vital role in the development of the area during the 19th century.

Tavern and Inn: Dunham Tavern served as a tavern and inn during the 1800s, making it a central hub for travelers, settlers, and local residents. The museum provides insights into the daily life of those who passed through or stayed at the tavern.

Historical Furnishings: The museum is typically furnished with period-appropriate items and artifacts, giving visitors a sense of what life was like in the 1800s. You can explore rooms furnished with early American furniture, textiles, and domestic objects.

Guided Tours: Visitors often take guided tours of the museum, led by knowledgeable docents or interpreters. These tours provide historical context and anecdotes about the tavern's history and its significance in the community.

Gardens and Grounds: The Dunham Tavern Museum typically has well-maintained gardens and outdoor spaces that showcase historical gardening practices and plantings from the 19th century.

Educational Programs: The museum may offer educational programs, workshops, and events related to early American history, craftsmanship, and daily life in the 1800s. These programs can offer a deeper understanding of the era.

Special Events: Check the museum's official website or event calendar for information on special events, historical reenactments, and programs that may be hosted throughout the year.

Accessibility: Museums often strive to provide accessibility for all visitors, including those with disabilities. Be sure to inquire about specific accommodations you may need.

Hours and Admission: Check the Dunham Tavern Museum's official website for current hours of operation, admission fees, membership options, and any special exhibitions or events.

Visiting the Dunham Tavern Museum is a journey back in time to the early days of Cleveland's history. Whether you have an interest in local history, early American life, or simply enjoy exploring historic sites, this museum offers an educational and immersive experience for visitors of all backgrounds and ages.

44. Attend the Cleveland National Air Show.

Attending the Cleveland National Air Show is a thrilling experience that allows you to witness incredible aerial displays, aviation feats, and military aircraft demonstrations. Here's what you can expect when you participate in this exciting event:

Travel to Cleveland Ohio

Aerial Performances: The Cleveland National Air Show typically features a lineup of spectacular aerial performances by skilled pilots and aviation teams. You can watch breathtaking aerobatic maneuvers, high-speed flybys, and gravity-defying stunts performed by both civilian and military aircraft.

Military Aircraft Displays: The air show often includes static displays of military aircraft, offering an up-close look at fighter jets, transport planes, helicopters, and other military aviation assets. It's an opportunity to see these impressive machines firsthand and learn about their capabilities.

Historical Aircraft: In addition to modern aircraft, you may find historical and vintage aircraft on display. These classic planes provide a glimpse into the history of aviation and may include World War II-era aircraft, biplanes, and more.

Parachute Teams: Some air shows feature parachute teams that perform daring jumps from high altitudes, often accompanied by pyrotechnics and precision landing demonstrations.

Jet Car Performances: Jet car performances are a crowd favorite, with powerful jet-propelled vehicles racing down the runway at incredible speeds.

Interactive Exhibits: Air shows often have interactive exhibits and displays related to aviation and aerospace. You can explore educational exhibits, learn about flight technology, and engage with aerospace professionals.

Food and Refreshments: The air show typically offers a variety of food vendors and concessions, allowing you to enjoy a meal or snack while watching the aerial displays.

Family-Friendly Activities: Air shows are family-friendly events, and you can often find activities for children, including aviation-themed games, face painting, and more.

Photo Opportunities: Whether you're a professional photographer or simply enjoy taking snapshots, air shows provide fantastic opportunities for capturing stunning aviation photographs.

Safety Measures: Event organizers prioritize safety, and you can expect to see security measures in place, including crowd control, first aid stations, and emergency response teams.

Accessibility: Air shows typically strive to provide accessibility for all visitors, including those with disabilities. Inquire about specific accommodations you may need.

Dates and Location: Check the Cleveland National Air Show's official website or local event listings for information on the event's dates, location, admission fees, parking details, and any special attractions or performers.

Attending the Cleveland National Air Show is an exhilarating experience that allows you to marvel at the capabilities of aircraft, witness incredible aerial displays, and appreciate the dedication and skill of pilots and aviation professionals. Whether you're an aviation enthusiast or simply looking for a day of excitement, this air show offers an unforgettable adventure in the world of flight.

45. Go kayaking on the Cuyahoga River.

Kayaking on the Cuyahoga River in Cleveland offers a scenic and adventurous way to explore the city's waterways and enjoy the outdoors. Here's what you can expect when you go kayaking on the Cuyahoga River:

Scenic Views: The Cuyahoga River flows through various parts of Cleveland, offering picturesque views of the city skyline, natural landscapes, and urban areas. You'll have the opportunity to see the city from a unique perspective.

Rental Options: Several outfitters and kayak rental companies operate along the Cuyahoga River, providing kayaks, paddles, and life jackets for rent. Whether you're an experienced kayaker or a beginner, you can typically find rental options suitable for your skill level.

Guided Tours: Some outfitters offer guided kayak tours, led by knowledgeable guides who can provide insights into the river's history, ecology, and points of interest. Guided tours can enhance your kayaking experience with educational information and local stories.

Paddling Routes: There are various paddling routes along the Cuyahoga River, each offering a unique experience. You can choose routes that take you through tranquil natural areas, past historic sites, or along urban waterfronts.

Travel to Cleveland Ohio

Wildlife Viewing: The Cuyahoga River and its surrounding areas are home to a variety of wildlife. While kayaking, keep an eye out for birds, fish, turtles, and other wildlife that inhabit the river and its banks.

Water Conditions: Be aware of water conditions, including current strength and water levels, which can vary depending on the time of year and recent weather. Always follow safety guidelines provided by outfitters and wear appropriate safety gear.

Photography Opportunities: Kayaking provides excellent opportunities for photography. You can capture stunning shots of the river, cityscape, and natural surroundings.

Relaxation and Recreation: Kayaking on the Cuyahoga River is a great way to relax, unwind, and enjoy the serenity of the water. It's also a form of outdoor recreation that allows you to stay active and connect with nature.

Accessibility: Outfitters typically provide kayaks and equipment suitable for individuals with varying levels of physical ability. Inquire about accessibility options if needed.

Hours and Reservations: Check with kayak rental companies for their hours of operation and reservation policies. It's a good idea to make reservations in advance, especially during peak kayaking season.

Kayaking on the Cuyahoga River offers a blend of urban and natural beauty, making it a popular activity for both locals and visitors. Whether you're looking for a peaceful paddle, a scenic adventure, or a new way to experience Cleveland, kayaking on the Cuyahoga River provides a memorable and enjoyable outdoor experience.

46. Visit the Baseball Heritage Museum.

Visiting the Baseball Heritage Museum in Cleveland is a journey through the history and cultural significance of baseball in America. Here's what you can expect when you explore this museum:

Celebrating Baseball History: The Baseball Heritage Museum is dedicated to preserving and celebrating the history of baseball, particularly its deep-rooted connection to the city of Cleveland and the broader American experience.

Exhibits and Artifacts: The museum typically features a collection of exhibits and artifacts that highlight the evolution of baseball, its impact on society, and the role of Cleveland in the sport's history. You can explore vintage baseball memorabilia, photographs, uniforms, equipment, and more.

Cleveland Baseball: The museum places a special emphasis on the history of baseball in Cleveland, including the city's rich tradition of professional baseball teams, players, and fans. You can learn about the Cleveland Indians (now the Guardians) and their contributions to the sport.

Negro League Baseball: Many baseball heritage museums, including this one, recognize the significant role of Negro League Baseball in American sports history. You can explore exhibits and stories related to the Negro Leagues and the African American baseball pioneers.

Educational Programs: The Baseball Heritage Museum may offer educational programs, workshops, and events related to baseball history, including lectures, discussions, and presentations by baseball historians and enthusiasts.

Special Exhibitions: Check the museum's official website or event calendar for information on special exhibitions, rotating displays, and temporary exhibits that may be featured throughout the year.

Interactive Displays: Some museums offer interactive displays and exhibits that engage visitors, allowing them to explore baseball's impact on culture, society, and the lives of players and fans.

Baseball Memorabilia: If you're a baseball enthusiast or collector, you may find vintage baseball cards, autographed items, and other memorabilia available for purchase or display.

Gift Shop: The museum typically has a gift shop where you can purchase baseball-themed merchandise, books, apparel, and souvenirs.

Accessibility: Museums often strive to provide accessibility for all visitors, including those with disabilities. Be sure to inquire about specific accommodations you may need.

Hours and Admission: Check the Baseball Heritage Museum's official website for current hours of operation, admission fees, membership options, and any special events or exhibitions.

Visiting the Baseball Heritage Museum is a chance to connect with the passion, history, and nostalgia of America's pastime. Whether you're a die-hard baseball fan, a history buff, or simply interested in the cultural impact of sports, this museum offers an engaging and enlightening experience for visitors of all backgrounds and ages.

47.Explore the Greater Cleveland Aquarium.

Exploring the Greater Cleveland Aquarium offers a fascinating underwater journey through aquatic ecosystems and marine life. Here's what you can expect when you visit this popular attraction:

Aquatic Exhibits: The Greater Cleveland Aquarium features a variety of aquatic exhibits that showcase marine life from around the world. These exhibits often include displays of fish, sharks, rays, turtles, and other underwater creatures.

Walkthrough Tunnels: One of the highlights of the aquarium is the walkthrough tunnels that allow you to get up close to marine life as they swim above and around you. These tunnels provide a unique and immersive underwater experience.

Local and Global Habitats: The aquarium typically showcases both local aquatic ecosystems, such as those found in Lake Erie, and global habitats like tropical rainforests and coral reefs. You can learn about the diverse environments that marine life calls home.

Touch Tanks: Some aquariums have touch tanks where visitors can interact with and touch marine animals like stingrays or sea stars under the guidance of trained staff.

Educational Programs: The Greater Cleveland Aquarium may offer educational programs, presentations, and demonstrations by marine biologists and educators. These programs provide insights into marine biology, conservation efforts, and the importance of protecting aquatic environments.

Children's Activities: Many aquariums offer children's play areas, educational games, and interactive exhibits designed to engage younger visitors and teach them about marine life.

Conservation Initiatives: Some aquariums have conservation initiatives and displays that highlight efforts to protect and preserve marine ecosystems and endangered species.

Special Events: Check the aquarium's official website or event calendar for information on special events, animal feedings, behind-the-scenes tours, and seasonal exhibits that may be offered.

Gift Shop: The aquarium typically has a gift shop where you can purchase aquatic-themed merchandise, souvenirs, and marine-related books and toys.

Accessibility: Aquariums often strive to provide accessibility for all visitors, including those with disabilities. Be sure to inquire about specific accommodations you may need.

Hours and Admission: Check the Greater Cleveland Aquarium's official website for current hours of operation, admission fees, membership options, and any special events or promotions.

Visiting the Greater Cleveland Aquarium offers a chance to explore the wonders of the underwater world, learn about marine ecosystems, and appreciate the diversity of marine life. Whether you have a passion for oceanography, marine biology, or simply enjoy the beauty of aquatic creatures, this aquarium provides an educational and captivating experience for visitors of all ages.

48. Attend a performance at the Beck Center for the Arts.

Attending a performance at the Beck Center for the Arts in Cleveland is a cultural and artistic experience that allows you to enjoy a wide range of theatrical and musical productions. Here's what you can expect when you attend a performance at this renowned arts center:

Theatrical Productions: The Beck Center for the Arts typically hosts a diverse lineup of theatrical performances, including plays, musicals, dramas, comedies, and classics. These productions often feature talented actors, directors, and designers who bring compelling stories to life on stage.

Travel to Cleveland Ohio

Musical Performances: In addition to theater, the Beck Center often presents musical performances, including concerts, recitals, and showcases featuring local and regional musicians, singers, and bands. You can enjoy a variety of musical genres, from classical and jazz to contemporary and folk.

Dance Performances: Some productions may include dance performances, ballets, or contemporary dance showcases. These events showcase the artistry and skill of local dance companies and choreographers.

Children's and Family Shows: The Beck Center often offers family-friendly productions and shows designed for children and young audiences. These performances provide an opportunity for families to enjoy the arts together.

Community Involvement: The Beck Center actively involves the community, and you may find productions that feature local actors and volunteers alongside professional artists. This creates a sense of community engagement and support for the arts.

Educational Programs: The center may offer educational programs, acting workshops, and theater classes for individuals of all ages interested in honing their performing arts skills.

Art Gallery: Some arts centers have on-site art galleries that feature rotating exhibitions of visual art, allowing you to explore various forms of artistic expression.

Accessibility: The Beck Center typically provides accessibility for all patrons, including those with disabilities. Inquire about specific accommodations you may need.

Ticketing and Reservations: To attend a performance, you'll need to purchase tickets in advance. Check the Beck Center's official website for information on ticket availability, show schedules, pricing, and any special promotions.

Café and Concessions: Many arts centers have on-site cafes or concessions where you can enjoy refreshments before or after a performance.

Hours of Operation: The center's operating hours can vary based on the performance schedule, so it's advisable to check the official website or contact the center for specific showtimes and details.

Attending a performance at the Beck Center for the Arts is an opportunity to immerse yourself in the world of live theater, music, and dance. Whether you're a theater enthusiast, a music lover, or simply seeking a memorable cultural experience, this arts center provides a platform for artistic expression and entertainment in the heart of Cleveland's vibrant arts community.

49. Take a ride on the Euclid Beach Park Grand Carousel.

Taking a ride on the Euclid Beach Park Grand Carousel is a nostalgic and enchanting experience that allows you to step back in time and enjoy a classic amusement park attraction. Here's what you can expect when you ride the Grand Carousel:

Historical Significance: The Euclid Beach Park Grand Carousel is a historic carousel that dates back to the early 20th century. It has been meticulously preserved to retain its original charm and craftsmanship.

Hand-Carved Wooden Horses: The centerpiece of the carousel is its hand-carved wooden horses, which are exquisitely detailed and beautifully painted. Each horse is a work of art in itself, making the carousel a true masterpiece of craftsmanship.

Organ Music: As you ride the carousel, you'll likely be serenaded by the melodious tones of a traditional band organ. The music adds to the nostalgic and whimsical atmosphere of the ride.

Riding Experience: The Grand Carousel offers a classic riding experience as you sit atop one of the wooden horses and go round and round. It's a delightful and family-friendly ride suitable for all ages.

Charming Setting: The carousel is often set within a charming pavilion or building, enhancing the overall atmosphere and providing shelter from the elements.

Nostalgic Feel: Riding the Euclid Beach Park Grand Carousel evokes a sense of nostalgia for a bygone era when amusement parks were a popular destination for families and friends.

Accessibility: Amusement parks and carousels typically aim to provide accessibility for all visitors, including those with disabilities. Be sure to inquire about specific accommodations you may need.

Ticketing: The cost of riding the carousel may vary, so it's a good idea to check with the amusement park or location where it is situated for information on ticket prices and operating hours.

Operating Season: The carousel may have specific operating seasons or hours, particularly if it is located within an amusement park or historic site. Check with the venue for the carousel's schedule.

Riding the Euclid Beach Park Grand Carousel is not only an enjoyable and timeless experience but also an opportunity to appreciate the artistry and craftsmanship of a bygone era. It's a ride that brings smiles to the faces of riders young and old, making it a cherished part of Cleveland's history and culture.

50. Visit the Cleveland Police Historical Society and Museum.

Visiting the Cleveland Police Historical Society and Museum provides insight into the history of law enforcement in Cleveland and showcases the contributions of the police force to the community. Here's what you can expect when you explore this museum:

Law Enforcement History: The museum is dedicated to preserving and presenting the history of the Cleveland Police Department and the evolution of law enforcement in the city. You can learn about the department's formation, early years, and its role in shaping the community.

Exhibits and Artifacts: The museum typically features a range of exhibits and artifacts related to policing, including historical uniforms, equipment, weapons, photographs, documents, and memorabilia. These displays offer a glimpse into the daily life and challenges of police officers throughout the years.

Historical Archives: Some police museums have extensive archives that house documents, case files, records, and photographs related to notable events, investigations, and law enforcement personnel. Researchers and historians may find these resources valuable.

Community Engagement: The Cleveland Police Historical Society and Museum often engage with the community by providing educational programs, outreach events, and safety demonstrations. These initiatives aim to foster positive relationships between law enforcement and the public.

Educational Programs: The museum may offer educational programs, workshops, and presentations on topics related to law enforcement, crime prevention, and public safety. These programs can be informative and engaging for visitors of all ages.

Historical Vehicles: Some police museums include displays of historical police vehicles, such as patrol cars and motorcycles, providing a look at the evolution of police transportation.

Interactive Exhibits: To enhance the visitor experience, some museums offer interactive exhibits that allow you to learn about police procedures, forensic science, and crime-solving techniques.

Gift Shop: The museum typically has a gift shop where you can purchase police-themed merchandise, books on law enforcement, and souvenirs.

Accessibility: Museums often strive to provide accessibility for all visitors, including those with disabilities. Be sure to inquire about specific accommodations you may need.

Hours and Admission: Check the Cleveland Police Historical Society and Museum's official website for current hours of operation, admission fees, membership options, and any special events or exhibitions.

Visiting this museum is an opportunity to gain a deeper understanding of the role of law enforcement in the community, learn about the history of policing in Cleveland, and appreciate the dedication and service of police officers. Whether you have an interest in law enforcement, criminal justice, or local history, this museum offers an educational and informative experience for visitors of all backgrounds.

Travel to Cleveland Ohio

51. Attend the Cleveland International Tattoo.

Attending the Cleveland International Tattoo is a vibrant and patriotic experience that celebrates the rich tradition of military and civilian tattoos. Here's what you can expect when you participate in this annual event:

Tattoo Performances: The Cleveland International Tattoo typically features a series of performances by military bands, pipe and drum corps, dance groups, and other talented performers. These acts showcase their musical and artistic skills in a grand spectacle.

Military Precision: Tattoos often highlight military precision, discipline, and traditions. You can expect to see elaborate drill routines, flag presentations, and ceremonial performances that pay homage to the armed forces.

Bagpipes and Drums: Many tattoos include stirring performances by bagpipe and drum corps. The haunting melodies of bagpipes and the rhythmic beats of drums create a powerful and emotional experience.

Dance and Cultural Performances: Some tattoos incorporate dance troupes and cultural performances that showcase the diversity and heritage of different regions and communities.

Massed Bands: One of the highlights of a tattoo is the massed bands performance, where multiple military and civilian bands come together to create a wall of sound. This synchronized musical display is a sight and sound to behold.

Military Pageantry: Tattoos often feature military pageantry with color guards, honor guards, and displays of flags and national symbols. These elements add a sense of ceremony and tradition to the event.

Community Engagement: Tattoos can involve the local community, with opportunities for local schools, youth groups, and organizations to participate in the event. This fosters a sense of civic pride and engagement.

Patriotic Spirit: The Cleveland International Tattoo typically evokes a strong sense of patriotism and pride, as it honors the sacrifices and contributions of military personnel and veterans.

Audience Participation: Depending on the format of the tattoo, there may be opportunities for audience participation, such as singing along with patriotic songs or joining in on certain traditions.

Accessibility: Event organizers often aim to provide accessibility for all attendees, including those with disabilities. Inquire about specific accommodations you may need.

Ticketing: Check the event's official website or ticketing platform for information on ticket availability, pricing, and seating options. Tickets for tattoos may sell out quickly, so it's advisable to plan ahead.

Dates and Venue: Be sure to verify the event's dates and venue, as they may change from year to year. Consult the official website or event listings for the most up-to-date information.

Attending the Cleveland International Tattoo is a memorable experience that combines music, culture, and tradition in a grand and patriotic celebration. Whether you have a connection to the military, an appreciation for music and performance, or simply enjoy community events, the tattoo offers an inspiring and unifying experience for audiences of all backgrounds.

52.Explore the Soldiers' and Sailors' Monument.

Exploring the Soldiers' and Sailors' Monument in Cleveland is an opportunity to pay tribute to the sacrifices of veterans and learn about the history of the American Civil War. Here's what you can expect when you visit this iconic monument:

Historical Significance: The Soldiers' and Sailors' Monument was erected to honor the soldiers and sailors from Cuyahoga County who served in the American Civil War (1861-1865). It stands as a symbol of gratitude and remembrance for their contributions.

Monument Design: The monument is a striking example of Civil War monument architecture. It features a 125-foot-tall column topped with a statue of the Goddess of Freedom. The column is surrounded by various sculptures, reliefs, and plaques that depict scenes from the Civil War.

Travel to Cleveland Ohio

Educational Exhibits: Inside the monument, you'll often find a museum with educational exhibits and displays related to the Civil War. These exhibits provide historical context, stories of local veterans, and information about the war's impact on the region.

Interactive Displays: Some monuments incorporate interactive displays and multimedia presentations that allow visitors to learn more about the Civil War through immersive experiences.

Observation Deck: The Soldiers' and Sailors' Monument may include an observation deck at the top, which offers panoramic views of downtown Cleveland and the surrounding area. It's an opportunity to see the city from a unique vantage point.

Memorial Plaza: The monument is typically surrounded by a memorial plaza with walkways, benches, and additional sculptures that pay tribute to various branches of the military and their contributions.

Veterans' Names: The monument often includes lists of the names of soldiers and sailors from Cuyahoga County who served in the Civil War. These names are inscribed on plaques or walls, creating a powerful and personal connection to history.

Ceremonial Events: The Soldiers' and Sailors' Monument serves as a focal point for various ceremonial events and patriotic gatherings throughout the year, including Veterans Day and Memorial Day commemorations.

Accessibility: Monuments often strive to provide accessibility for all visitors, including those with disabilities. Be sure to inquire about specific accommodations you may need.

Hours and Admission: Check the Soldiers' and Sailors' Monument's official website or contact them for current hours of operation, admission fees (if any), and any special events or programs.

Visiting the Soldiers' and Sailors' Monument is a way to honor the legacy of those who served during the Civil War and gain a deeper understanding of this pivotal period in American history. Whether you're interested in history, veterans' memorials, or simply seeking a reflective and educational experience, this monument offers a poignant and memorable visit for visitors of all backgrounds and ages.

53. Visit the Dittrick Medical History Center.

Visiting the Dittrick Medical History Center in Cleveland provides a unique opportunity to explore the history of medicine, healthcare, and the fascinating world of medical artifacts. Here's what you can expect when you visit this center:

Historical Medical Collections: The Dittrick Medical History Center houses extensive collections of medical artifacts, instruments, documents, and rare books dating back to the 18th century. These collections offer insights into the evolution of medical practices, technologies, and research.

Medical Instruments: You can expect to see a wide array of medical instruments and devices used by physicians and surgeons throughout history. These include surgical tools, diagnostic equipment, and instruments used in various medical specialties.

Rare Books and Manuscripts: The center often has a library with rare medical books, manuscripts, and medical journals that provide historical perspectives on medical knowledge, research, and education.

Medical Artifacts: The museum may display medical artifacts, such as anatomical models, apothecary tools, and early pharmaceutical items. These artifacts offer a glimpse into the practice of medicine in different eras.

Educational Exhibits: The Dittrick Medical History Center often features educational exhibits and displays that explore specific themes in medical history, medical innovations, and the social and cultural aspects of healthcare.

Medical Imaging: Some centers showcase the evolution of medical imaging technologies, from early X-rays to modern imaging techniques, demonstrating how these advancements have transformed diagnosis and treatment.

Medical Ethics and Social Issues: Exhibits may also delve into topics related to medical ethics, social issues in healthcare, and the impact of medical advancements on society.

Interactive Displays: To engage visitors, some centers offer interactive displays and hands-on activities that allow you to explore medical instruments and concepts firsthand.

Archival Research: The center may provide resources and support for researchers, historians, and scholars interested in studying medical history and related topics.

Accessibility: Museums and centers often strive to provide accessibility for all visitors, including those with disabilities. Inquire about specific accommodations you may need.

Hours and Admission: Check the Dittrick Medical History Center's official website or contact them for current hours of operation, admission fees (if any), and any special events or programs.

Visiting the Dittrick Medical History Center is a chance to journey through the history of medicine, from early practices to modern advancements. Whether you have a keen interest in medical history, healthcare innovations, or the intersection of science and society, this center offers a thought-provoking and educational experience for visitors of all backgrounds and interests.

54. Attend the Feast of the Assumption in Little Italy.

Attending the Feast of the Assumption in Cleveland's Little Italy is a vibrant and culturally rich experience that celebrates Italian heritage, food, and traditions. Here's what you can expect when you participate in this annual event:

Religious Celebration: The Feast of the Assumption is a religious festival that honors the Assumption of the Blessed Virgin Mary into heaven, a significant event in Catholic tradition. The festival often includes religious processions, blessings, and ceremonies.

Cultural Festival: In addition to its religious significance, the Feast of the Assumption has evolved into a lively cultural festival that showcases Italian and Italian-American heritage. You can immerse yourself in the vibrant traditions, music, and customs of Italy.

Food and Cuisine: One of the highlights of the Feast is the abundance of Italian cuisine. You can savor a wide variety of Italian dishes, including pasta, pizza, cannoli, gelato, and other delectable treats. Food vendors and local restaurants offer a diverse selection of Italian delicacies.

Street Fair: The festival typically features a lively street fair with vendors selling Italian-themed merchandise, arts and crafts, clothing, and souvenirs. It's an excellent opportunity for shopping and discovering unique Italian products.

Live Music and Entertainment: The Feast often hosts live music performances, including Italian folk music, traditional dances, and contemporary bands. You can enjoy the festive atmosphere with music and entertainment throughout the event.

Children's Activities: Families can find children's activities and amusements, such as carnival rides, games, face painting, and kid-friendly entertainment.

Processions and Parades: Processions and parades are a central part of the Feast, with religious icons and statues carried through the streets. These processions are often accompanied by traditional music and prayers.

Religious and Cultural Exhibits: Some festivals include exhibits or displays related to Italian religious artifacts, traditions, and the history of Little Italy in Cleveland.

Art and Craft Demonstrations: You may have the opportunity to watch artisans and craftsmen demonstrate traditional Italian arts and crafts, such as pottery, painting, or woodworking.

Accessibility: Event organizers often aim to provide accessibility for all attendees, including those with disabilities. Inquire about specific accommodations you may need.

Dates and Location: The Feast of the Assumption typically takes place in Cleveland's Little Italy neighborhood. Be sure to check the official event website or local listings for the most up-to-date information on dates, times, and specific activities.

Attending the Feast of the Assumption is a delightful way to experience the warmth and hospitality of Little Italy while celebrating Italian culture and traditions. Whether you're a food enthusiast, a lover of music and dance, or

Travel to Cleveland Ohio

simply looking to enjoy a cultural festival, this event offers a memorable and joyful experience for visitors of all backgrounds and ages.

55. Explore the Cleveland Skating Club.

Exploring the Cleveland Skating Club offers an opportunity to experience the world of figure skating and ice sports in a historic and elegant setting. Here's what you can expect when you visit this club:

Figure Skating and Ice Sports: The Cleveland Skating Club is primarily a hub for figure skating and ice sports enthusiasts. You can observe or participate in figure skating sessions, ice hockey, synchronized skating, and other ice-related activities. The club often hosts training sessions for skaters of all ages and skill levels.

Historic Venue: The club is known for its historic and beautiful venue, which may include an ice rink surrounded by ornate architecture, grand chandeliers, and a classic ambiance. The historic setting adds to the charm and elegance of the skating experience.

Competitions and Shows: The Cleveland Skating Club frequently hosts figure skating competitions, exhibitions, and ice shows featuring local and international skaters. These events showcase the artistry and athleticism of figure skating.

Skating Lessons: Whether you're a beginner or an experienced skater, the club often offers skating lessons and coaching for individuals and groups. Skating instructors can help you improve your skills and technique.

Ice Dancing: Ice dancing is a popular activity at the club, and you may have the opportunity to watch or participate in ice dance classes and sessions.

Membership: The club typically offers membership options for individuals and families interested in becoming part of the skating community. Members often have access to exclusive events, ice time, and club facilities.

Events and Social Activities: In addition to skating, the club may host social events, parties, and gatherings for members and their families. It's a chance to connect with others who share a passion for ice sports.

Facilities: Beyond the ice rink, the club may offer amenities such as a club lounge, pro shop, locker rooms, and a warm and inviting atmosphere for skaters and spectators alike.

Accessibility: Clubs generally strive to provide accessibility for all members and visitors, including those with disabilities. Inquire about specific accommodations you may need.

Hours of Operation: Check the Cleveland Skating Club's official website or contact them for current hours of operation, ice time schedules, and any special events or programs.

Visiting the Cleveland Skating Club is an opportunity to appreciate the grace and skill of figure skaters, experience the thrill of ice sports, and enjoy the camaraderie of a community passionate about skating. Whether you're an aspiring skater, a fan of ice sports, or simply looking for an elegant and unique recreational experience, this club offers a welcoming and enjoyable atmosphere for all ages.

56. Take a tour of the Federal Reserve Bank of Cleveland.

Taking a tour of the Federal Reserve Bank of Cleveland provides a fascinating glimpse into the world of central banking, monetary policy, and the operations of one of the regional banks within the Federal Reserve System. Here's what you can expect when you visit:

Educational Experience: The tour typically offers an educational experience that includes an overview of the Federal Reserve System, its history, and its role in the U.S. economy. You'll learn about the structure and functions of the Federal Reserve.

Monetary Policy: You can expect to gain insights into monetary policy and the tools the Federal Reserve uses to manage the nation's money supply, interest rates, and economic stability. The tour may cover topics like inflation, interest rates, and the Federal Open Market Committee (FOMC).

Banking Operations: The tour often includes a behind-the-scenes look at the various operations of the Cleveland Federal Reserve Bank, including the

Travel to Cleveland Ohio

processing of currency, coin, and checks. You may see the high-tech machinery used to authenticate and process money.

Economic Data: Some tours feature discussions on economic data and research conducted by the Federal Reserve, helping you understand how economic data influences policy decisions.

Financial Education: The Federal Reserve Bank may offer financial education programs and resources that promote financial literacy and economic understanding for visitors of all ages.

Interactive Exhibits: To enhance the learning experience, there may be interactive exhibits, displays, and multimedia presentations that explain complex economic concepts in a user-friendly way.

Security Measures: Given the importance of the Federal Reserve's role in the economy, you can expect to encounter security measures and protocols designed to protect the integrity of the bank's operations.

Q&A Session: Tours often include a question-and-answer session, allowing visitors to ask questions about central banking, monetary policy, and the Federal Reserve's role in the economy.

Accessibility: The Federal Reserve typically strives to provide accessibility for all visitors, including those with disabilities. Be sure to inquire about specific accommodations you may need.

Reservation: It's advisable to check the Federal Reserve Bank of Cleveland's official website or contact them in advance to make reservations for a tour, as they may have specific tour times and visitor requirements.

Identification: As a federal institution, you may be required to show valid identification to enter the facility.

Restrictions: Note that there may be restrictions on photography, recording, or the use of electronic devices during the tour. Be sure to follow any guidelines provided by the Federal Reserve staff.

A tour of the Federal Reserve Bank of Cleveland offers an educational and informative experience that demystifies the world of central banking and monetary policy. Whether you're a student, an economist, or simply interested in how the financial system works, this tour provides valuable insights into the functions and responsibilities of the Federal Reserve in maintaining the stability of the U.S. economy.

57. Attend the Tri-C JazzFest.

Attending the Tri-C JazzFest in Cleveland is a fantastic way to immerse yourself in the world of jazz music and experience live performances by talented musicians. Here's what you can expect when you participate in this annual jazz festival:

Live Jazz Performances: The Tri-C JazzFest typically features a diverse lineup of jazz artists and ensembles performing various styles of jazz music, including traditional, contemporary, fusion, and more. You can enjoy live concerts by both established and emerging jazz musicians.

World-Class Artists: The festival often attracts renowned jazz musicians, Grammy-winning artists, and jazz legends who deliver captivating performances. It's an opportunity to witness exceptional talent on stage.

Multiple Stages: JazzFest may have multiple stages and venues where performances take place simultaneously. This allows you to explore different styles of jazz and discover new artists.

Educational Programs: In addition to live music, JazzFest often includes educational programs such as workshops, masterclasses, and discussions led by jazz experts and musicians. These programs offer insights into the artistry and history of jazz.

Jam Sessions: Some festivals host jam sessions or open mic events where local and visiting musicians can come together to create spontaneous jazz performances. These sessions can be a lot of fun and provide a sense of community.

Food and Beverages: JazzFest typically offers a variety of food vendors, concessions, and beverage options, allowing you to enjoy delicious cuisine while listening to jazz.

Art and Merchandise: You'll often find art exhibits, jazz-themed merchandise, and vendor booths selling jazz recordings, books, and memorabilia. It's a great place to pick up souvenirs and support artists.

Family-Friendly Activities: Some jazz festivals include family-friendly activities, such as interactive music stations for children and families, ensuring that jazz appreciation spans generations.

Accessibility: Event organizers often aim to provide accessibility for all attendees, including those with disabilities. Inquire about specific accommodations you may need.

Ticketing: Check the official Tri-C JazzFest website or ticketing platforms for information on ticket availability, pricing, and any special packages or discounts.

Dates and Location: Be sure to verify the festival's dates and venue, as they may change from year to year. Consult the official website or local listings for the most up-to-date information.

Attending the Tri-C JazzFest is a memorable experience that allows you to celebrate the rich heritage and innovation of jazz music. Whether you're a jazz enthusiast, a music lover, or someone looking for an enjoyable cultural event, this festival offers a vibrant and engaging celebration of the art form.

58. Go to a Cleveland Monsters hockey game.

Attending a Cleveland Monsters hockey game is an exciting way to experience professional ice hockey in Cleveland. Here's what you can expect when you go to a Monsters game:

American Hockey League (AHL): The Cleveland Monsters are a professional ice hockey team that competes in the American Hockey League (AHL), which is one of the top minor leagues in North American hockey. The team is affiliated with the National Hockey League's (NHL) Columbus Blue Jackets.

Game Atmosphere: Monsters games typically feature an energetic and passionate fan base, creating a thrilling atmosphere in the arena. The games are family-friendly and suitable for fans of all ages.

Game Schedule: The AHL season typically runs from October to April, with home and away games. Be sure to check the team's official website or the AHL website for the current season's schedule, including game dates, opponents, and start times.

Quicken Loans Arena: The Monsters play their home games at Quicken Loans Arena, which is also known as Rocket Mortgage FieldHouse. The arena offers modern amenities, comfortable seating, and excellent sightlines for hockey fans.

Concessions: Arena concessions provide a variety of food and beverage options, including traditional hockey game fare like hot dogs, nachos, and popcorn. You can enjoy a meal or snack while watching the game.

Merchandise: Team merchandise, including jerseys, hats, and other Monsters apparel, is typically available for purchase at the arena, allowing you to support the team and take home souvenirs.

Intermission Entertainment: Hockey games often feature entertainment during intermissions, such as fan contests, promotions, and opportunities to win prizes.

Accessibility: Arena facilities are designed to be accessible to all visitors, including those with disabilities. Inquire about specific accommodations you may need.

Ticketing: Tickets for Monsters games can be purchased through the team's official website, the arena's box office, or authorized ticket vendors. It's a good idea to secure your tickets in advance, especially for popular matchups.

Fan Engagement: Monsters games provide opportunities for fan engagement, from cheering on the team to participating in crowd chants and traditions. The team mascot often interacts with fans, adding to the excitement.

Parking: Quicken Loans Arena typically offers parking options for attendees. Be sure to check the arena's website or contact them for information on parking facilities and fees.

Attending a Cleveland Monsters hockey game is a thrilling experience, whether you're a die-hard hockey fan or just looking for a fun night out. You can witness the fast-paced action on the ice, soak in the lively atmosphere, and be part of the enthusiastic crowd as you support the team.

Travel to Cleveland Ohio

59. Visit the William G. Mather Museum.

Visiting the William G. Mather Museum in Cleveland offers a unique opportunity to explore the history of Great Lakes shipping and maritime heritage. Here's what you can expect when you visit this museum:

Historical Significance: The William G. Mather Museum is situated on the retired Great Lakes freighter SS William G. Mather, which once transported iron ore and coal on the Great Lakes. The ship itself is a part of the museum's historical collection.

Tour of the Ship: Visitors to the museum can typically take a guided or self-guided tour of the SS William G. Mather. Exploring the ship provides insights into the working conditions and daily life of sailors on the Great Lakes.

Maritime Exhibits: The museum often includes exhibits and displays related to the maritime history of the Great Lakes, featuring artifacts, photographs, models, and memorabilia. You can learn about the ships, industries, and communities that depended on Great Lakes shipping.

Cargo Hold: A visit to the cargo hold of the ship allows you to see the massive cargo compartments where iron ore, coal, and other materials were transported. The cargo hold often features informative displays about the freighter's operations.

Engine Room: Some tours take you into the engine room of the SS William G. Mather, where you can see the ship's powerful engines and machinery up close.

Crew Quarters: You may have the opportunity to explore the crew's quarters, including sleeping quarters, the galley (kitchen), and communal spaces. This offers a glimpse into the daily life of sailors.

Navigational Equipment: Exhibits may showcase navigational equipment, including maps, charts, and instruments used for safely navigating the Great Lakes.

Interactive Displays: To engage visitors, the museum may offer interactive displays and hands-on activities related to maritime history, ship navigation, and Great Lakes geography.

Educational Programs: Some museums host educational programs, workshops, and special events related to maritime history, making it an informative experience for all ages.

Accessibility: Museums often strive to provide accessibility for all visitors, including those with disabilities. Inquire about specific accommodations you may need.

Hours and Admission: Check the William G. Mather Museum's official website or contact them for current hours of operation, admission fees, and any special events or programs.

Visiting the William G. Mather Museum is an opportunity to step back in time and appreciate the vital role that Great Lakes shipping played in the industrial and economic development of the region. Whether you have an interest in maritime history, engineering, or simply enjoy exploring unique museums, this museum aboard a historic freighter offers a memorable and educational experience for visitors of all backgrounds.

60.Explore the Warther Museum and Gardens.

Exploring the Warther Museum and Gardens in Dover, Ohio, provides a unique opportunity to appreciate the intricate artistry of Ernest "Mooney" Warther and explore beautifully landscaped gardens. Here's what you can expect when you visit this museum:

Ernest "Mooney" Warther's Carvings: The museum is dedicated to showcasing the incredible hand-carved artwork of Ernest "Mooney" Warther. Mooney was a master carver who created intricate, functional wooden pliers entirely from wood and without the use of nails, screws, or glue. His carvings are displayed throughout the museum and provide a fascinating look at his craftsmanship and creativity.

Plier Trees: One of the highlights of the museum is Mooney Warther's collection of plier trees, which display the evolution of his carvings. These trees feature hundreds of his wooden pliers, each carved with exceptional precision and attention to detail.

Travel to Cleveland Ohio

Knife Collections: In addition to the pliers, the museum often features displays of Mooney Warther's knife collection, including beautifully crafted knives with intricate handles. Mooney was a skilled knife maker, and his knife designs are renowned for their artistry.

Family History: The museum may provide insights into the history of the Warther family, including Mooney's life and the legacy of his craftsmanship. You can learn about his upbringing, family traditions, and the artistic journey that led to his creations.

Gardens: Surrounding the museum is a lush and meticulously maintained garden area that includes a variety of plants, flowers, and shrubs. Strolling through the gardens offers a peaceful and visually appealing experience.

Educational Displays: The Warther Museum often features educational displays that explain the techniques and processes used by Mooney Warther in his carving and knife-making endeavors.

Guided Tours: Guided tours of the museum are typically available, providing visitors with in-depth information about Mooney Warther's life, art, and the significance of his creations.

Gift Shop: The museum may have a gift shop where you can purchase souvenirs, including replicas of Mooney Warther's pliers, knives, and other related items.

Accessibility: Museums often strive to provide accessibility for all visitors, including those with disabilities. Be sure to inquire about specific accommodations you may need.

Hours and Admission: Check the Warther Museum and Gardens' official website or contact them for current hours of operation, admission fees, and any special events or programs.

Visiting the Warther Museum and Gardens is a chance to admire the craftsmanship of an extraordinary artist, appreciate the beauty of meticulously maintained gardens, and learn about the history and legacy of the Warther family. Whether you have an interest in woodworking, art, or simply enjoy exploring unique museums and gardens, this museum offers an engaging and visually stunning experience for visitors of all backgrounds.

61. Attend the Cleveland Pride Parade and Festival.

Attending the Cleveland Pride Parade and Festival is a vibrant and celebratory experience that supports and promotes LGBTQ+ rights, equality, and diversity. Here's what you can expect when you participate in this annual event:

Pride Parade: The Cleveland Pride Parade is a colorful and joyful procession that typically features a diverse array of participants, including LGBTQ+ individuals, allies, organizations, and supporters. Expect to see vibrant floats, decorated vehicles, marching bands, community groups, and individuals expressing their pride through costumes and signs.

Route: The parade route may wind through downtown Cleveland, and spectators often line the streets to cheer on participants. Check the official event website or local listings for specific route details and timing.

Festival: Following the parade, the Cleveland Pride Festival usually takes place in a central location. The festival offers a lively atmosphere with music, entertainment, food vendors, and community booths. You can explore a variety of LGBTQ+-focused organizations, businesses, and resources.

Live Entertainment: The festival often hosts live performances by local and national artists, drag performers, dance groups, and musicians. These performances add to the festive ambiance and celebration of LGBTQ+ culture.

Vendor Booths: You'll find vendor booths offering LGBTQ+ merchandise, rainbow-themed items, clothing, accessories, and information about LGBTQ+ support services and organizations.

Food and Refreshments: A diverse range of food vendors typically offers a variety of culinary delights, including international cuisine, local specialties, and festival favorites.

Family-Friendly Activities: Some Pride festivals include family-friendly activities, such as children's areas, games, and interactive experiences suitable for all ages.

Community Engagement: The event often provides opportunities for attendees to connect with LGBTQ+ organizations, advocacy groups, and community leaders who work to advance LGBTQ+ rights and inclusion.

Accessibility: Pride events typically strive to be inclusive and accessible to all attendees, including those with disabilities. Inquire about specific accommodations you may need.

Dates and Location: Be sure to check the official Cleveland Pride Parade and Festival website or local listings for the most up-to-date information on dates, festival hours, and the festival's location.

Participating in the Cleveland Pride Parade and Festival is a chance to celebrate diversity, promote acceptance, and show solidarity with the LGBTQ+ community. Whether you identify as LGBTQ+ or as an ally, attending this event allows you to join in the spirit of inclusion and support for equal rights and love in all its forms.

62. Visit the Cleveland Hungarian Heritage Society.

Visiting the Cleveland Hungarian Heritage Society provides an opportunity to explore the rich cultural heritage of the Hungarian community in Cleveland and its contributions to the region. Here's what you can expect when you visit this heritage society:

Cultural Exhibits: The Cleveland Hungarian Heritage Society typically features exhibits that showcase the history, traditions, and cultural artifacts of the Hungarian community in Cleveland. These exhibits may include photographs, documents, artwork, and memorabilia that highlight the experiences of Hungarian immigrants and their descendants in the region.

Art and Folklore: You may have the opportunity to explore Hungarian art and folklore through displays of traditional costumes, crafts, music, dance, and other forms of cultural expression. These exhibits provide insights into the vibrant traditions of Hungary.

Educational Programs: The heritage society often hosts educational programs, lectures, and workshops related to Hungarian history, language, cuisine, and customs. These programs offer visitors the chance to learn more about Hungary and its cultural heritage.

Genealogy and Research: Some heritage societies provide resources for genealogical research, helping individuals trace their Hungarian ancestry and family histories.

Library and Archives: The society may have a library or archives that house books, documents, and records related to Hungarian history and culture. Researchers and history enthusiasts can access these resources for scholarly and genealogical purposes.

Events and Celebrations: Throughout the year, the heritage society may organize cultural events, festivals, and celebrations that showcase Hungarian traditions, holidays, and cuisine. These events often feature music, dance performances, and delicious Hungarian food.

Gift Shop: Visitors can often find a gift shop where they can purchase Hungarian-themed items, books, music, and souvenirs that celebrate Hungarian culture.

Community Engagement: The heritage society serves as a hub for the local Hungarian community, fostering connections and preserving cultural ties among Hungarian Americans. Visitors can engage with members and learn about community activities and initiatives.

Accessibility: Heritage societies generally strive to provide accessibility for all visitors, including those with disabilities. Inquire about specific accommodations you may need.

Hours and Admission: Check the Cleveland Hungarian Heritage Society's official website or contact them for current hours of operation, admission fees, and any special events or programs.

Visiting the Cleveland Hungarian Heritage Society is an opportunity to appreciate the enduring cultural contributions of the Hungarian community in Cleveland and gain a deeper understanding of Hungary's history and traditions. Whether you have Hungarian roots or simply have an interest in world cultures, this heritage society offers an enriching and educational experience for visitors of all backgrounds and ages.

Travel to Cleveland Ohio

63. Go to a Cleveland Gladiators arena football game.

Attending a Cleveland Gladiators arena football game is an exhilarating experience that combines fast-paced sports action with an electric atmosphere. Here's what you can expect when you go to a Gladiators game:

Arena Football: The Cleveland Gladiators are a professional arena football team that competes in the Indoor Football League (IFL). Arena football is a high-scoring and fast-paced version of American football, played indoors in a smaller arena.

Game Atmosphere: Gladiators games are known for their exciting and fan-friendly atmosphere. The close proximity to the field and the intimate arena setting make for an immersive and up-close fan experience.

Quicken Loans Arena: The Gladiators typically play their home games at Quicken Loans Arena, which is also known as Rocket Mortgage FieldHouse. The arena provides excellent sightlines, comfortable seating, and modern amenities for fans.

Game Schedule: The IFL season typically runs from spring to early summer, with a schedule of home and away games. Be sure to check the team's official website or the IFL website for the current season's schedule, including game dates, opponents, and start times.

Fan Engagement: Gladiators games often feature fan engagement activities, including halftime shows, promotions, contests, and opportunities to interact with the team mascot and cheerleaders.

Concessions: Arena concessions offer a variety of food and beverage options, allowing you to enjoy classic stadium fare while watching the game.

Merchandise: Team merchandise, including Gladiators jerseys, hats, and other apparel, is typically available for purchase at the arena, allowing you to show your support for the team.

Accessibility: Arena facilities are designed to be accessible to all visitors, including those with disabilities. Inquire about specific accommodations you may need.

Ticketing: Tickets for Gladiators games can be purchased through the team's official website, the arena's box office, or authorized ticket vendors. It's a good idea to secure your tickets in advance, especially for popular matchups.

Parking: Quicken Loans Arena typically offers parking options for attendees. Be sure to check the arena's website or contact them for information on parking facilities and fees.

Attending a Cleveland Gladiators arena football game is a thrilling experience, whether you're a passionate football fan, a sports enthusiast, or someone looking for an exciting live entertainment option. You can witness the fast-paced action on the field, enjoy the camaraderie of fellow fans, and be part of the electrifying energy that arena football games offer.

64.Explore the Ukrainian Museum-Archives.

Exploring the Ukrainian Museum-Archives in Cleveland is a fascinating journey into the history, culture, and heritage of the Ukrainian community in Northeast Ohio. Here's what you can expect when you visit this museum:

Cultural Exhibits: The Ukrainian Museum-Archives typically features exhibits that highlight the history, traditions, and contributions of the Ukrainian diaspora in the region. These exhibits may include artifacts, photographs, documents, artworks, and memorabilia that offer insights into the Ukrainian-American experience.

Art and Folklore: Visitors can often explore Ukrainian art and folklore through displays of traditional costumes, embroidery, religious icons, pottery, and other forms of cultural expression. The museum showcases the rich artistic traditions of Ukraine.

Educational Programs: The museum frequently hosts educational programs, lectures, and workshops related to Ukrainian history, language, cuisine, and customs. These programs provide visitors with opportunities to learn about Ukraine and its cultural heritage.

Archival Resources: As an archives facility, the museum may house an extensive collection of documents, records, manuscripts, and photographs related to Ukrainian history, immigration, and community life. Researchers and genealogists can access these resources for scholarly and genealogical research.

Library: Some museums have a library that includes books, publications, and reference materials related to Ukrainian culture, history, and literature. Visitors interested in learning more about Ukraine may find valuable resources here.

Community Engagement: The Ukrainian Museum-Archives serves as a focal point for the local Ukrainian community, fostering connections and preserving cultural ties among Ukrainian Americans. Visitors can engage with members and learn about community activities and initiatives.

Gift Shop: The museum often has a gift shop where you can purchase Ukrainian-themed items, books, music, art, and souvenirs that celebrate Ukrainian culture.

Accessibility: Museums generally strive to provide accessibility for all visitors, including those with disabilities. Inquire about specific accommodations you may need.

Hours and Admission: Check the Ukrainian Museum-Archives' official website or contact them for current hours of operation, admission fees, and any special events or programs.

Visiting the Ukrainian Museum-Archives is an opportunity to appreciate the enduring cultural contributions of the Ukrainian community in Cleveland and gain a deeper understanding of Ukraine's history and traditions. Whether you have Ukrainian heritage or simply have an interest in world cultures, this museum offers an enriching and educational experience for visitors of all backgrounds and ages.

65. Attend the Cleveland Kurentovanje Festival.

Attending the Cleveland Kurentovanje Festival is a lively and culturally enriching experience that celebrates Slovenian traditions, folklore, and the coming of spring. Here's what you can expect when you participate in this annual event:

Kurent Characters: The festival centers around the Kurent, a traditional Slovenian character known for chasing away winter and evil spirits with its colorful and elaborate costume. You can expect to see individuals dressed as Kurent characters, complete with large masks, sheepskin jackets, and bells, creating a visually striking spectacle.

Parade: Kurentovanje often features a festive parade where Kurent characters, as well as other traditional Slovenian and cultural groups, march through the streets of Cleveland. The parade is a highlight of the festival and typically includes music, dancing, and vibrant costumes.

Live Music and Performances: The festival typically offers live music performances, traditional Slovenian folk music, dance groups, and entertainment on multiple stages. You can enjoy a diverse range of musical genres and cultural expressions.

Food and Cuisine: Slovenian cuisine takes center stage at Kurentovanje. You can savor traditional Slovenian dishes and delicacies, such as krofi (doughnuts), sausages, potica (nut roll), and other tasty treats. Food vendors often serve these delicious offerings.

Crafts and Artisans: The festival may host craft vendors and artisans showcasing handmade Slovenian crafts, traditional clothing, jewelry, and art. It's an opportunity to explore and purchase unique items.

Interactive Activities: Kurentovanje often includes interactive activities for all ages, such as workshops, children's games, and cultural displays. These activities provide a hands-on experience of Slovenian culture.

Cultural Exhibits: Visitors can often explore exhibits and displays that highlight Slovenian history, customs, and heritage. These exhibits offer insights into the Slovenian-American community in Cleveland.

Beer and Beverages: You can enjoy a variety of beverages, including Slovenian beer, wine, and other refreshments. Beer gardens and beverage stations are typically part of the festival.

Accessibility: Event organizers often aim to provide accessibility for all attendees, including those with disabilities. Be sure to inquire about specific accommodations you may need.

Travel to Cleveland Ohio

Dates and Location: Be sure to check the official Cleveland Kurentovanje Festival website or local listings for the most up-to-date information on dates, festival hours, and the festival's location.

Participating in the Cleveland Kurentovanje Festival is an opportunity to immerse yourself in Slovenian culture, traditions, and the joyful spirit of spring. Whether you have Slovenian heritage or simply appreciate cultural festivals, Kurentovanje offers a lively and engaging experience for visitors of all backgrounds and ages.

66. Take a scenic drive along the Lake Erie Coastal Ohio Trail.

Taking a scenic drive along the Lake Erie Coastal Ohio Trail is a picturesque journey that offers breathtaking views of Lake Erie, charming coastal towns, and a variety of natural landscapes. Here's what you can expect when you embark on this scenic drive:

Stunning Lake Views: As you drive along the Lake Erie Coastal Ohio Trail, you'll be treated to stunning panoramic views of Lake Erie. The lake's blue waters stretch as far as the eye can see, creating a serene and tranquil backdrop for your journey.

Coastal Towns: The route typically passes through several charming coastal towns and communities, each with its own unique character and attractions. These towns often offer opportunities to explore local shops, restaurants, and historical sites.

Lighthouses: Along the way, you may encounter historic lighthouses that dot the Lake Erie shoreline. These lighthouses are not only functional but also serve as iconic landmarks and great photo opportunities.

Beaches and Parks: The drive often takes you near beautiful beaches and waterfront parks where you can stop and relax, have a picnic, or take a leisurely walk along the shore. Some areas may offer opportunities for swimming and water sports.

Scenic Byways: The Lake Erie Coastal Ohio Trail may follow designated scenic byways, which are specifically chosen for their picturesque landscapes and attractions. These byways provide a well-marked and enjoyable route.

Birdwatching: Lake Erie is known for its diverse bird population, especially during migration seasons. Birdwatchers may spot various species of waterfowl and migratory birds along the coast.

Fishing: Lake Erie is a popular destination for anglers, and you may come across fishing piers and marinas where you can cast a line or observe local fishermen in action.

Winery Visits: Some sections of the trail pass through Ohio's wine country, where you can visit wineries and vineyards, sample local wines, and enjoy scenic views of the vine-covered landscapes.

Cultural and Historical Sites: The route may include stops at cultural and historical attractions, such as museums, historic sites, and landmarks that offer insights into the region's heritage.

Accessibility: Scenic byways and routes often strive to be accessible to all travelers, including those with disabilities. Inquire about specific accommodations you may need.

Maps and Guides: Before embarking on your journey, consider obtaining maps or guides that provide information about the Lake Erie Coastal Ohio Trail, including recommended stops, attractions, and accommodations.

Safety: Be mindful of traffic regulations, speed limits, and road conditions as you enjoy the drive. Ensure that you have essential items like a map, GPS device, and a fully charged phone for navigation and emergencies.

The Lake Erie Coastal Ohio Trail offers a memorable and visually stunning driving experience that allows you to connect with nature, explore coastal communities, and appreciate the beauty of Lake Erie's shoreline. Whether you're a nature enthusiast, a road trip lover, or simply seeking a scenic adventure, this coastal drive is sure to leave you with lasting memories.

67.Go horseback riding in the Metroparks.

Going horseback riding in the Cleveland Metroparks is a wonderful way to enjoy the natural beauty of the area while experiencing the thrill of horseback

Travel to Cleveland Ohio

riding. Here's what you can expect when you go horseback riding in the Metroparks:

Trails: The Cleveland Metroparks typically offers a network of scenic trails suitable for horseback riding. These trails wind through wooded areas, open meadows, and along the banks of rivers and streams, providing a variety of natural landscapes to explore.

Trail Difficulty: The Metroparks usually designates trails of varying difficulty levels, from easy to more challenging, to accommodate riders of different skill levels. Whether you're a beginner or an experienced equestrian, you can find a trail that suits your abilities.

Scenic Views: While riding, you'll have the opportunity to take in scenic views of the park's diverse ecosystems, wildlife habitats, and the natural beauty of the region. Keep an eye out for local wildlife, such as deer, birds, and other creatures.

Guided Tours: Some Metroparks may offer guided horseback riding tours led by experienced trail guides. These tours provide informative insights into the park's natural history, ecology, and points of interest.

Equestrian Facilities: Many Metroparks have dedicated equestrian facilities, including parking areas, hitching posts, and restrooms to make your horseback riding experience more convenient and enjoyable.

Accessibility: Parks generally aim to provide accessibility for all visitors, including those with disabilities. Inquire about specific accommodations you may need for horseback riding.

Riding Regulations: Be sure to familiarize yourself with any park rules and regulations related to horseback riding, including trail etiquette, safety guidelines, and any permit requirements.

Equipment: You'll need to have appropriate riding gear, including a well-fitting helmet, suitable riding attire, and riding boots. If you don't have your own horse, inquire with the park or local stables about rental options.

Hours: Check the Cleveland Metroparks' official website or contact them for information on park hours, trail availability, and any special events related to horseback riding.

Before heading out for a horseback riding adventure in the Metroparks, it's a good idea to plan your route, ensure your horse is adequately prepared, and take any necessary safety precautions. Whether you're a seasoned rider or a beginner, exploring the Metroparks on horseback offers a peaceful and immersive way to connect with nature and appreciate the scenic beauty of the region.

68. Visit the Dittrick Medical History Center.

Visiting the Dittrick Medical History Center in Cleveland offers a captivating journey into the history of medicine and healthcare. Here's what you can expect when you explore this unique institution:

Medical History Exhibits: The Dittrick Medical History Center typically features exhibits that showcase the evolution of medicine and healthcare over the centuries. These exhibits may include medical instruments, surgical tools, anatomical models, and artifacts from various eras.

Rare Collections: The center houses an extensive collection of rare books, manuscripts, and archives related to the history of medicine and medical practices. Researchers and history enthusiasts can delve into these collections to explore the development of medical knowledge and techniques.

Medical Artifacts: Visitors can often view a wide range of medical artifacts, including antique medical devices, pharmaceutical items, and historical documents. These artifacts provide insights into the practice of medicine in different time periods.

Medical Illustrations: The Dittrick Medical History Center frequently displays medical illustrations and artwork that have been instrumental in documenting and teaching medical procedures and anatomical knowledge.

Educational Programs: The center often hosts educational programs, lectures, and workshops that delve into various aspects of medical history. These programs are designed to engage visitors and provide a deeper understanding of the field.

Library and Research: Some medical history centers offer library and research facilities where scholars and enthusiasts can access medical literature, journals, and reference materials related to the history of medicine.

Travel to Cleveland Ohio

Accessibility: Institutions like the Dittrick Medical History Center typically strive to provide accessibility for all visitors, including those with disabilities. Inquire about specific accommodations you may need.

Hours and Admission: Check the center's official website or contact them for current hours of operation, admission fees, and any special events or exhibitions.

Visiting the Dittrick Medical History Center is an opportunity to appreciate the progress and innovations in the field of medicine, learn about the history of medical practices, and gain a deeper understanding of the challenges and breakthroughs that have shaped healthcare over the centuries. Whether you have a background in medicine or simply have an interest in the history of science, this center offers an enlightening and educational experience for visitors of all backgrounds and ages.

69. Attend the Cleveland Museum of Natural History's Think & Drink series.

Attending the Cleveland Museum of Natural History's Think & Drink series is an engaging and intellectually stimulating experience that combines discussions, lectures, and social interaction with a focus on science and natural history. Here's what you can expect when you participate in this thought-provoking event:

Educational Discussions: The Think & Drink series typically features discussions, lectures, and presentations led by experts, scientists, and scholars on various topics related to natural history, biology, geology, and other scientific fields. These sessions offer a platform for in-depth exploration and learning.

Interactive Conversations: Attendees have the opportunity to engage in interactive conversations with speakers and fellow participants. These discussions often encourage critical thinking and the exchange of ideas.

Themes and Topics: Each Think & Drink event may have a specific theme or topic, such as evolution, environmental conservation, astronomy, or paleontology. The content is designed to be informative, thought-provoking, and relevant to contemporary scientific issues.

Evening Setting: Think & Drink sessions are often held in the evening, creating a relaxed and social atmosphere. Attendees can enjoy refreshments and beverages while participating in the discussions.

Networking: The events provide an excellent opportunity for networking with fellow science enthusiasts, academics, and professionals who share an interest in natural history and scientific discovery.

Accessibility: The museum typically strives to provide accessibility for all attendees, including those with disabilities. Inquire about specific accommodations you may need.

Tickets and Registration: To attend a Think & Drink event, you may need to purchase tickets or register in advance. Check the Cleveland Museum of Natural History's official website or contact them for information on upcoming sessions, ticket availability, and registration details.

Schedule: Think & Drink events are often scheduled periodically throughout the year. Be sure to check the museum's event calendar for the most up-to-date information on upcoming sessions and topics.

Participating in the Cleveland Museum of Natural History's Think & Drink series offers a unique opportunity to delve into scientific exploration, engage with experts in the field, and connect with a community of individuals who share a passion for natural history and scientific discovery. Whether you're a scientist, a science enthusiast, or simply curious about the world around you, this series provides an intellectually rewarding and enjoyable experience.

70. Explore the Italian Cultural Garden.

Exploring the Italian Cultural Garden in Cleveland is a delightful experience that allows you to immerse yourself in Italian culture, art, and natural beauty. Here's what you can expect when you visit this cultural garden:

Beautiful Garden Setting: The Italian Cultural Garden is typically a well-maintained garden that showcases Italian landscape design, horticulture, and artistic elements. It offers a serene and picturesque setting for visitors to enjoy.

Italian Sculptures and Statues: Within the garden, you can often find Italian sculptures, statues, and artistic installations that pay homage to Italian culture,

Travel to Cleveland Ohio

history, and renowned figures. These sculptures are not only aesthetically pleasing but also offer educational and cultural insights.

Walkways and Paths: The garden typically features pathways and walkways that wind through various sections, allowing visitors to explore the garden at their own pace. These paths often lead to different themed areas or highlight different aspects of Italian culture.

Floral Displays: Depending on the season, you may encounter a variety of colorful and fragrant flowers and plants that contribute to the garden's beauty. The selection of plantings may reflect Italian flora and horticultural traditions.

Cultural Symbols: Look for cultural symbols and elements that represent Italy's rich heritage, including symbols of art, music, literature, and architecture. These symbols can provide a deeper understanding of Italy's cultural contributions to the world.

Educational Signage: The garden may feature informative signage that provides historical context and explanations of the sculptures, statues, and cultural references found throughout the garden.

Photography Opportunities: The Italian Cultural Garden offers numerous photo opportunities, making it a popular spot for both amateur and professional photographers.

Events and Performances: The garden occasionally hosts cultural events, performances, and gatherings related to Italian heritage. These events may include music, dance, art exhibitions, and festivals.

Accessibility: Cultural gardens typically aim to provide accessibility for all visitors, including those with disabilities. Inquire about specific accommodations you may need.

Hours and Admission: Check the Italian Cultural Garden's official website or contact them for information on hours of operation, admission fees, and any special events or programs.

Visiting the Italian Cultural Garden is an opportunity to appreciate the enduring cultural contributions of Italy, enjoy the beauty of a well-tended garden, and gain a deeper understanding of Italian heritage. Whether you have Italian roots, an interest in art and culture, or simply appreciate beautiful outdoor spaces, this cultural garden offers an enriching and visually pleasing experience for visitors of all backgrounds and ages.

71. Take a cooking class at the Loretta Paganini School of Cooking.

Taking a cooking class at the Loretta Paganini School of Cooking in Cleveland is a delicious and educational experience for food enthusiasts of all skill levels. Here's what you can expect when you enroll in a cooking class at this renowned culinary school:

Professional Instruction: The Loretta Paganini School of Cooking is led by experienced and talented chefs who provide expert instruction. They'll guide you through the cooking process, offering tips, techniques, and culinary insights.

Diverse Class Offerings: The school typically offers a wide range of cooking classes, covering various cuisines, cooking styles, and skill levels. Classes may focus on Italian cuisine, baking and pastry, gourmet cooking, ethnic dishes, and more. You can choose a class that aligns with your interests and goals.

Hands-On Experience: Most classes are hands-on, allowing you to actively participate in preparing dishes from start to finish. You'll have the opportunity to chop, sauté, roast, and plate your creations under the guidance of the chef instructor.

Recipes and Techniques: In addition to preparing dishes, you'll receive detailed recipes and instructions that you can take home and replicate in your own kitchen. These recipes often include tips and techniques to help you master the dishes.

Tasting and Enjoyment: After the cooking is complete, you'll have the pleasure of enjoying the dishes you've prepared. Many classes conclude with a meal where you can savor the flavors of your culinary creations.

Group Setting: Cooking classes are typically conducted in a group setting, providing an opportunity to socialize, interact with fellow food enthusiasts, and share your passion for cooking.

Kitchen Facilities: The school is equipped with professional-grade kitchen facilities and modern cooking equipment, providing an authentic and well-equipped cooking environment.

Special Events: The Loretta Paganini School of Cooking may also host special events, guest chef appearances, and themed cooking experiences throughout the year. These events offer unique culinary experiences.

Gift Certificates: Cooking classes at the school can make excellent gifts for friends and family who love to cook. Gift certificates are often available for purchase.

Registration: To attend a cooking class, you typically need to register in advance through the school's website or by contacting them directly. Check the school's schedule for upcoming classes, availability, and registration details.

Whether you're a novice cook looking to build fundamental skills or an experienced cook seeking to expand your culinary repertoire, a cooking class at the Loretta Paganini School of Cooking is a fun and rewarding way to enhance your cooking abilities and indulge in your passion for food.

72. Visit the Cleveland Hungarian Heritage Museum.

Visiting the Cleveland Hungarian Heritage Museum provides a unique opportunity to explore the rich cultural heritage and history of the Hungarian community in Cleveland and its contributions to the region. Here's what you can expect when you visit this museum:

Cultural Exhibits: The Cleveland Hungarian Heritage Museum typically features exhibits that highlight the history, traditions, and contributions of the Hungarian diaspora in the region. These exhibits may include artifacts, photographs, documents, artworks, and memorabilia that offer insights into the Hungarian-American experience.

Art and Folklore: Visitors can often explore Hungarian art and folklore through displays of traditional costumes, embroidery, religious icons, pottery, and other forms of cultural expression. The museum showcases the rich artistic traditions of Hungary.

Educational Programs: The museum frequently hosts educational programs, lectures, and workshops related to Hungarian history, language, cuisine, and customs. These programs provide visitors with opportunities to learn about Hungary and its cultural heritage.

Archival Resources: As a heritage museum, the institution may have an extensive collection of documents, records, manuscripts, and photographs related to Hungarian history, immigration, and community life. Researchers and genealogists can access these resources for scholarly and genealogical research.

Library: Some museums have a library that includes books, publications, and reference materials related to Hungarian culture, history, and literature. Visitors interested in learning more about Hungary may find valuable resources here.

Community Engagement: The Cleveland Hungarian Heritage Museum serves as a hub for the local Hungarian community, fostering connections and preserving cultural ties among Hungarian Americans. Visitors can engage with members and learn about community activities and initiatives.

Gift Shop: The museum often has a gift shop where you can purchase Hungarian-themed items, books, music, art, and souvenirs that celebrate Hungarian culture.

Accessibility: Museums generally strive to provide accessibility for all visitors, including those with disabilities. Inquire about specific accommodations you may need.

Hours and Admission: Check the Cleveland Hungarian Heritage Museum's official website or contact them for current hours of operation, admission fees, and any special events or programs.

Visiting the Cleveland Hungarian Heritage Museum is an opportunity to appreciate the enduring cultural contributions of the Hungarian community in Cleveland and gain a deeper understanding of Hungary's history and traditions. Whether you have Hungarian roots or simply have an interest in world cultures, this museum offers an enriching and educational experience for visitors of all backgrounds and ages.

Travel to Cleveland Ohio

73. Attend the Cleveland Labor Day Oktoberfest.

Attending the Cleveland Labor Day Oktoberfest is a festive and lively way to celebrate the holiday weekend with German-inspired food, music, and culture. Here's what you can expect when you participate in this annual event:

German Cuisine: The Oktoberfest typically features a wide array of delicious German cuisine, including bratwurst, sauerkraut, schnitzel, pretzels, potato salad, and other traditional dishes. You can savor authentic German flavors and enjoy hearty meals.

Beer and Beverages: Oktoberfest is known for its beer offerings, and you can usually find a variety of German and domestic beers, including Oktoberfest-style brews. Raise a stein and toast to the festivities. Non-alcoholic beverages are also available.

Live Music and Entertainment: The event often hosts live music performances by German bands and folk musicians, creating a lively and festive atmosphere. You can expect to hear polka music, traditional German songs, and dance tunes.

Dance and Entertainment: Oktoberfest typically includes dance performances, including traditional German folk dances. You may even have the chance to join in on the dancing and enjoy the vibrant atmosphere.

Children's Activities: Family-friendly activities are usually part of the celebration, with options for kids such as games, rides, and craft activities. It's an excellent way for families to enjoy the event together.

Cultural Exhibits: You can often explore exhibits and displays that showcase German culture, history, and traditions. Learn about the heritage and contributions of the German-American community in Cleveland.

Vendors and Artisans: The festival often hosts vendors selling German-themed merchandise, crafts, and souvenirs. It's a great opportunity to shop for unique items.

Accessibility: Event organizers typically aim to provide accessibility for all attendees, including those with disabilities. Inquire about specific accommodations you may need.

Tickets and Admission: Check the official Cleveland Labor Day Oktoberfest website or contact the event organizers for information on admission fees, ticket options, and any special promotions or discounts.

Dates and Location: Be sure to check the event's official website or local listings for the most up-to-date information on dates, festival hours, and the event's location.

The Cleveland Labor Day Oktoberfest is a beloved annual tradition that allows you to experience the vibrant and welcoming spirit of German culture. Whether you have German heritage or simply enjoy cultural festivals, this event offers a fun and memorable way to celebrate Labor Day weekend with friends and family.

74. Explore the Estonian Cultural Garden.

Exploring the Estonian Cultural Garden in Cleveland is a wonderful opportunity to immerse yourself in Estonian culture, history, and natural beauty. Here's what you can expect when you visit this cultural garden:

Beautiful Garden Setting: The Estonian Cultural Garden is typically a well-maintained garden that showcases Estonian landscape design, horticulture, and artistic elements. It offers a serene and picturesque setting for visitors to enjoy.

Estonian Art and Sculptures: Within the garden, you can often find Estonian sculptures, statues, and artistic installations that celebrate Estonian culture, history, and notable figures. These sculptures are not only visually appealing but also offer educational and cultural insights.

Walkways and Paths: The garden typically features pathways and walkways that wind through different sections, allowing visitors to explore the garden at their own pace. These paths often lead to different themed areas or highlight various aspects of Estonian culture.

Floral Displays: Depending on the season, you may encounter a variety of colorful and fragrant flowers and plants that contribute to the garden's beauty. The selection of plantings may reflect Estonian flora and horticultural traditions.

Cultural Symbols: Look for cultural symbols and elements that represent Estonia's rich heritage, including symbols of art, music, literature, and architecture. These symbols can provide a deeper understanding of Estonian cultural contributions to the world.

Educational Signage: The garden may feature informative signage that provides historical context and explanations of the sculptures, statues, and cultural references found throughout the garden.

Photography Opportunities: The Estonian Cultural Garden offers numerous photo opportunities, making it a popular spot for both amateur and professional photographers.

Accessibility: Cultural gardens typically aim to provide accessibility for all visitors, including those with disabilities. Inquire about specific accommodations you may need.

Hours and Admission: Check the Estonian Cultural Garden's official website or contact them for information on hours of operation, admission fees, and any special events or programs.

Visiting the Estonian Cultural Garden is an opportunity to appreciate the enduring cultural contributions of Estonia, enjoy the beauty of a well-tended garden, and gain a deeper understanding of Estonian heritage. Whether you have Estonian roots, an interest in art and culture, or simply appreciate beautiful outdoor spaces, this cultural garden offers an enriching and visually pleasing experience for visitors of all backgrounds and ages.

75. Go ziplining at Common Ground Canopy Tours.

Ziplining at Common Ground Canopy Tours is an exhilarating outdoor adventure that allows you to soar through the treetops and experience the thrill of flying. Here's what you can expect when you embark on a ziplining tour at Common Ground Canopy Tours:

Safety First: Before your ziplining adventure begins, you'll typically receive a safety briefing and be equipped with all the necessary safety gear, including a harness, helmet, and gloves. Trained guides will provide instructions on how to use the equipment safely.

Scenic Setting: Common Ground Canopy Tours is often located in a scenic natural environment, such as a forested area or park. As you zip from platform to platform, you'll have the opportunity to enjoy stunning views of the surrounding landscape and natural beauty.

Zipline Courses: Zipline courses at Common Ground Canopy Tours typically consist of a series of platforms connected by ziplines. You'll zip from one platform to another, often at varying heights and lengths, creating an exciting and memorable experience.

Variety of Lines: Depending on the course, you may encounter a variety of ziplines, including classic ziplines, canopy ziplines, and even some that allow you to race a friend or family member to the next platform.

Thrills and Excitement: Ziplining offers an adrenaline rush as you speed through the air. The feeling of flying and the wind rushing past you make it a thrilling activity that's suitable for adventure seekers.

Guided Tours: Ziplining tours at Common Ground Canopy Tours are typically guided experiences. Knowledgeable guides accompany you throughout the adventure, providing information about the local environment, wildlife, and ziplining techniques.

Accessibility: Ziplining tours often aim to accommodate a wide range of participants, including those with different levels of physical fitness. However, it's a good idea to inquire about any specific physical requirements or restrictions when booking your tour.

Reservations: It's advisable to make reservations in advance for your ziplining tour, especially during peak seasons, to secure your spot on the course.

Photography: Some ziplining tours offer the option to have photographs taken during your adventure, allowing you to capture the excitement and scenery.

Duration: The duration of a ziplining tour can vary depending on the course and the number of ziplines included. Plan for several hours of adventure.

Weather Considerations: Be aware that ziplining tours may be weather-dependent. It's a good idea to check with Common Ground Canopy Tours regarding their policy on inclement weather and rescheduling options.

Travel to Cleveland Ohio

Ziplining at Common Ground Canopy Tours is a memorable and adrenaline-pumping experience that allows you to connect with nature while enjoying an exciting adventure. Whether you're an experienced zipliner or trying it for the first time, it offers a unique perspective of the outdoors and a thrilling way to spend time in the great outdoors.

76. Visit the American Police Motorcycle Museum.

Visiting the American Police Motorcycle Museum in Meredith, New Hampshire, offers a unique opportunity to explore the history and evolution of police motorcycles and law enforcement in the United States. Here's what you can expect when you visit this museum:

Historical Police Motorcycles: The museum typically features a collection of vintage and historic police motorcycles from various eras. These motorcycles are often restored to their original condition and represent the development of police bike technology over the years.

Law Enforcement Memorabilia: In addition to motorcycles, you can often find a variety of law enforcement memorabilia, including uniforms, equipment, badges, and other artifacts that provide insights into the history and culture of policing in America.

Educational Exhibits: The museum may have educational exhibits that highlight the role of police motorcycles in law enforcement, as well as the stories of officers who rode them. These exhibits often offer historical context and information.

Interactive Displays: Some museums include interactive displays that allow visitors to learn about the mechanics and features of police motorcycles. You may have the chance to sit on a motorcycle or try out a simulated ride.

Audiovisual Presentations: Look for audiovisual presentations or documentaries that share the history and significance of police motorcycles and their role in maintaining public safety.

Accessibility: Museums typically aim to provide accessibility for all visitors, including those with disabilities. Inquire about specific accommodations you may need.

Gift Shop: The museum often has a gift shop where you can purchase law enforcement-themed items, souvenirs, and merchandise related to motorcycles and policing.

Hours and Admission: Check the American Police Motorcycle Museum's official website or contact them for information on hours of operation, admission fees, and any special events or programs.

Visiting the American Police Motorcycle Museum is a chance to appreciate the history of law enforcement in the United States and gain a deeper understanding of the role of motorcycles in policing. Whether you have an interest in law enforcement, motorcycles, or history, this museum offers an engaging and educational experience for visitors of all backgrounds and ages.

77. Explore the Slavic Village neighborhood.

Exploring the Slavic Village neighborhood in Cleveland, Ohio, allows you to discover a community with a rich history, diverse culture, and a variety of attractions. Here's what you can expect when you visit Slavic Village:

Historical Significance: Slavic Village is known for its historical significance as one of Cleveland's oldest and most culturally diverse neighborhoods. It was settled by Eastern European immigrants, particularly those of Slavic descent, in the late 19th and early 20th centuries.

Cultural Heritage: The neighborhood's heritage is still evident today through its cultural institutions, churches, and events that celebrate Slavic traditions. You may encounter festivals, cultural performances, and ethnic restaurants that showcase the neighborhood's heritage.

Historic Architecture: Slavic Village features a mix of historic architecture, including charming brick homes, churches, and other structures that reflect the architectural styles of the early 20th century. Take a walk or drive through the neighborhood to admire its unique character.

Museums and Cultural Centers: Depending on the season and current offerings, you might find cultural centers or museums in Slavic Village that offer insights into the neighborhood's history and heritage.

Travel to Cleveland Ohio

Parks and Green Spaces: The neighborhood may have parks and green spaces where you can relax, have a picnic, or enjoy outdoor activities. These spaces are often used for community gatherings and events.

Local Businesses: Explore the local businesses in the area, including bakeries, delis, and markets that offer authentic Slavic and Eastern European cuisine and products. It's an opportunity to taste traditional dishes and explore the neighborhood's culinary offerings.

Community Events: Slavic Village often hosts community events, festivals, and gatherings that bring residents and visitors together. These events may include live music, food vendors, and activities for all ages.

Art and Culture: Look for public art installations, murals, and cultural initiatives that highlight the neighborhood's artistic and creative side. Slavic Village may have a vibrant arts scene.

Accessibility: Slavic Village typically aims to provide accessibility for all visitors, including those with disabilities. Inquire about specific accommodations you may need.

Community Engagement: Consider reaching out to local community organizations or neighborhood associations to learn about upcoming events, volunteer opportunities, or ways to engage with the community during your visit.

Safety: While Slavic Village has made strides in revitalization efforts, it's advisable to exercise normal safety precautions when exploring any urban neighborhood, especially if you're unfamiliar with the area.

Slavic Village offers a unique blend of history, culture, and community spirit. Exploring this neighborhood provides a chance to connect with the traditions of its immigrant founders and to experience the vibrant culture that continues to thrive today. Whether you're interested in history, culture, or simply want to enjoy the atmosphere of a diverse neighborhood, Slavic Village has much to offer.

78. Attend the Serbian Cultural Garden's Serbian Festival.

Attending the Serbian Cultural Garden's Serbian Festival in Cleveland is a vibrant and cultural experience that allows you to immerse yourself in Serbian heritage, music, food, and traditions. Here's what you can expect when you participate in this annual festival:

Cultural Celebrations: The Serbian Festival typically celebrates Serbian culture, history, and traditions. It often includes cultural performances, music, dance, and displays of Serbian art and craftsmanship.

Live Music and Dance: You can enjoy live performances of traditional Serbian music and dance. Look for folk dance groups and musicians who showcase the lively and rhythmic aspects of Serbian culture.

Traditional Serbian Food: One of the highlights of the festival is the opportunity to savor authentic Serbian cuisine. Expect to find dishes such as cevapi (grilled sausages), sarma (cabbage rolls), pita (pastries), and various desserts. Serbian cuisine is known for its rich flavors and hearty offerings.

Crafts and Souvenirs: The festival often features vendors selling Serbian crafts, artwork, textiles, and souvenirs. It's a great place to shop for unique items and gifts.

Children's Activities: Many Serbian Festivals offer activities for children, such as games, rides, and craft stations. It's a family-friendly event where kids can learn about Serbian culture in an engaging way.

Cultural Exhibits: Explore exhibits that showcase Serbian history, art, and cultural contributions. These exhibits may include historical photographs, artifacts, and educational displays.

Community Engagement: The Serbian Festival is an opportunity to connect with members of the Serbian community in Cleveland. You can learn about their traditions, customs, and community organizations.

Accessibility: Event organizers typically aim to provide accessibility for all attendees, including those with disabilities. Inquire about specific accommodations you may need.

Travel to Cleveland Ohio

Tickets and Admission: Check the Serbian Cultural Garden's official website or contact the festival organizers for information on admission fees, ticket options, and any special promotions or discounts.

Dates and Location: Be sure to check the festival's official website or local listings for the most up-to-date information on dates, festival hours, and the event's location.

Attending the Serbian Festival in the Serbian Cultural Garden is a wonderful way to experience the warmth and hospitality of the Serbian community, enjoy traditional Serbian music and cuisine, and gain a deeper appreciation for Serbian culture and heritage. Whether you have Serbian roots or simply appreciate cultural festivals, this event offers a festive and enriching experience for visitors of all backgrounds and ages.

79. Take a scenic drive along the Covered Bridge Tour Route.

Taking a scenic drive along the Covered Bridge Tour Route is a picturesque journey that allows you to explore the charm and history of covered bridges in various locations. Here's what you can expect when you embark on this scenic drive:

Beautiful Scenery: The Covered Bridge Tour Route typically passes through scenic countryside, forests, and rural areas, providing stunning views of natural landscapes. Depending on the season, you may encounter lush greenery, vibrant autumn foliage, or serene winter scenes.

Historic Covered Bridges: The main attraction of the route is the covered bridges themselves. You'll have the opportunity to drive through, walk across, or admire these historic and iconic structures. Each covered bridge has its own unique design and history, offering a glimpse into the past.

Photography Opportunities: The route offers numerous opportunities for photography. Capture the charm of the covered bridges, the surrounding landscapes, and any wildlife or natural features you encounter along the way.

Local History: Many of the covered bridges have informational plaques or signs that provide details about their history, construction, and significance. You can learn about the communities that built and maintained these bridges over the years.

Scenic Byways: The route may include sections of scenic byways or country roads that are known for their beauty and tranquility. These roads often have lower speed limits, allowing you to leisurely enjoy the journey.

Seasonal Activities: Depending on the time of year, you may find seasonal activities along the route, such as farmers' markets, festivals, or roadside stands selling local produce and crafts.

Local Communities: The Covered Bridge Tour Route often passes through or near small towns and communities. Consider making stops to explore these charming areas, visit local shops, or enjoy a meal at a local restaurant.

Accessibility: Most covered bridges and scenic byways aim to provide accessibility for all visitors, including those with disabilities. Inquire about specific accommodations you may need.

Maps and Information: Before starting your journey, obtain maps, brochures, or information about the route, including the locations of covered bridges and any other points of interest.

Safety: Be aware of local traffic laws and safety guidelines, especially when driving through covered bridges. Some bridges may have size or weight restrictions, so plan your route accordingly.

The Covered Bridge Tour Route offers a peaceful and nostalgic journey through rural landscapes, where you can connect with history and appreciate the enduring beauty of covered bridges. Whether you're a history enthusiast, a nature lover, or simply seeking a scenic drive, this route provides a memorable and tranquil experience for travelers of all interests.

80. Visit the Greater Cleveland Aquarium's 230,000-gallon shark exhibit.

Visiting the Greater Cleveland Aquarium's 230,000-gallon shark exhibit is an exciting opportunity to explore the fascinating world of underwater life, including various species of sharks. Here's what you can expect when you visit this impressive exhibit:

Travel to Cleveland Ohio

Shark Species: The 230,000-gallon shark exhibit typically houses a variety of shark species. You can expect to see different types of sharks, each with its own unique characteristics and behaviors. Common species may include nurse sharks, sand tiger sharks, and more.

Observation Opportunities: The exhibit often features observation areas with large viewing windows that allow you to get up close and personal with the sharks and other marine life. You can watch these incredible creatures as they swim gracefully through the water.

Educational Signage: Look for informative signage and displays that provide details about the sharks, their habitats, and their role in marine ecosystems. You can learn about shark conservation efforts and the importance of protecting these apex predators.

Aquarium Staff: Knowledgeable aquarium staff and educators are often available to answer your questions and provide interesting insights into the behavior and biology of sharks. They may offer scheduled presentations or feedings that you can attend.

Additional Marine Life: The shark exhibit is often part of a larger aquarium complex that includes a wide range of marine life, such as fish, rays, turtles, and other creatures. You can explore various themed tanks and displays throughout the aquarium.

Interactive Exhibits: Some aquariums offer interactive exhibits related to shark biology, ocean conservation, and marine science. These hands-on displays provide an engaging and educational experience for visitors of all ages.

Conservation Messaging: Many aquariums use their exhibits as platforms to raise awareness about marine conservation issues, including the protection of sharks and their natural habitats. You may learn about efforts to conserve and protect these vital ocean species.

Accessibility: Aquariums typically aim to provide accessibility for all visitors, including those with disabilities. Inquire about specific accommodations you may need.

Hours and Admission: Check the Greater Cleveland Aquarium's official website or contact them for information on hours of operation, admission fees, and any special events or programs.

Visiting the shark exhibit at the Greater Cleveland Aquarium is an opportunity to appreciate the beauty and diversity of marine life, gain a better understanding of shark conservation, and witness these magnificent creatures in a controlled and educational setting. Whether you're a marine enthusiast or simply curious about the underwater world, the exhibit offers an immersive and awe-inspiring experience.

81. Attend the Cleveland One World Festival.

Attending the Cleveland One World Festival is a vibrant and multicultural experience that celebrates the diversity and unity of the city's various cultural communities. Here's what you can expect when you participate in this lively festival:

Cultural Performances: The One World Festival typically features a diverse lineup of cultural performances, including music, dance, and artistic expressions from around the world. You can enjoy traditional and contemporary performances that showcase the talents and cultural heritage of different communities.

Global Cuisine: One of the highlights of the festival is the opportunity to savor a wide variety of international cuisines. You can sample dishes from different countries and regions, ranging from street food to traditional favorites. It's a culinary journey that allows you to taste flavors from around the world.

Crafts and Artwork: The festival often hosts vendors selling crafts, artwork, textiles, and souvenirs from various cultures. It's a great place to shop for unique items and gifts while supporting local artisans and businesses.

Interactive Workshops: Look for interactive workshops and activities that offer hands-on experiences related to different cultures. These workshops may include arts and crafts, dance lessons, cooking demonstrations, and more.

Cultural Exhibits: Explore cultural exhibits that provide insights into the history, traditions, and contributions of different communities. These exhibits may include artifacts, photographs, and educational displays.

Travel to Cleveland Ohio

Children's Activities: Many One World Festivals offer activities for children, including games, face painting, storytelling, and educational activities that promote cultural understanding.

Community Engagement: The festival is an opportunity to connect with members of various cultural communities in Cleveland. You can learn about their traditions, customs, and community organizations, and engage in meaningful conversations.

Accessibility: Event organizers typically aim to provide accessibility for all attendees, including those with disabilities. Inquire about specific accommodations you may need.

Community Resources: Information booths and community resource centers may be available to provide information on local services, support networks, and opportunities for involvement in diverse communities.

Dates and Location: Be sure to check the festival's official website or local listings for the most up-to-date information on dates, festival hours, and the event's location.

The Cleveland One World Festival is a celebration of cultural diversity and a testament to the city's commitment to inclusivity. Whether you have a personal connection to a particular culture or simply appreciate the beauty of a multicultural society, this festival offers a lively and enriching experience for visitors of all backgrounds and ages. It's a reminder that, despite our differences, we are all part of one global community.

82. Explore the Slovenian Museum and Archives.

Exploring the Slovenian Museum and Archives in Cleveland offers a unique opportunity to delve into the rich cultural heritage and history of the Slovenian community in the city. Here's what you can expect when you visit this museum and archives:

Cultural Exhibits: The Slovenian Museum and Archives typically feature a wide range of cultural exhibits that highlight the history, traditions, and contributions of the Slovenian diaspora in Cleveland. These exhibits may include artifacts, photographs, documents, artworks, and memorabilia that provide insights into Slovenian culture and heritage.

Art and Folklore: Visitors can often explore Slovenian art and folklore through displays of traditional costumes, embroidery, religious icons, pottery, and other forms of cultural expression. The museum showcases the rich artistic traditions of Slovenia.

Archival Resources: As an archives facility, the institution may have an extensive collection of documents, records, manuscripts, and photographs related to Slovenian history, immigration, and community life. Researchers and genealogists can access these resources for scholarly and genealogical research.

Library: Some museums and archives have a library that includes books, publications, and reference materials related to Slovenian culture, history, and literature. Visitors interested in learning more about Slovenia may find valuable resources here.

Educational Programs: The museum and archives often host educational programs, lectures, and workshops related to Slovenian history, language, cuisine, and customs. These programs provide visitors with opportunities to learn about Slovenia and its cultural heritage.

Community Engagement: The Slovenian Museum and Archives serve as a hub for the local Slovenian community, fostering connections and preserving cultural ties among Slovenian Americans. Visitors can engage with members and learn about community activities and initiatives.

Accessibility: Museums and archives typically aim to provide accessibility for all visitors, including those with disabilities. Inquire about specific accommodations you may need.

Gift Shop: The museum may have a gift shop where you can purchase Slovenian-themed items, books, music, art, and souvenirs that celebrate Slovenian culture.

Hours and Admission: Check the Slovenian Museum and Archives' official website or contact them for current hours of operation, admission fees, and any special events or programs.

Travel to Cleveland Ohio

Visiting the Slovenian Museum and Archives is an opportunity to appreciate the enduring cultural contributions of the Slovenian community in Cleveland and gain a deeper understanding of Slovenia's history and traditions. Whether you have Slovenian roots or simply have an interest in world cultures, this museum and archives offer an enriching and educational experience for visitors of all backgrounds and ages.

83. Go on a wine tour of Ohio's wine country.

Embarking on a wine tour of Ohio's wine country is a delightful way to explore the state's winemaking heritage and sample a variety of local wines. Here's what you can expect when you go on a wine tour of Ohio's wine regions:

Scenic Vineyards: Ohio's wine country is often set in picturesque rural landscapes, featuring rolling vineyards, lush grapevines, and charming wineries. You'll have the opportunity to enjoy the natural beauty of the region as you visit different wineries.

Wine Tastings: Winery tours typically include wine tastings where you can sample a selection of wines produced by the winery. Depending on the winery, you may taste reds, whites, rosés, and even sparkling wines. Knowledgeable staff may guide you through the tasting, offering insights into the wines' characteristics.

Educational Tours: Many wineries offer guided tours of their facilities, allowing you to learn about the winemaking process from grape to bottle. You can see the production areas, barrel rooms, and wine cellars.

Winery Atmosphere: Each winery has its unique atmosphere and charm. Some may have cozy tasting rooms with fireplaces, outdoor patios, or picnic areas where you can relax and enjoy the scenery.

Food Pairings: Some wineries offer food pairings or have on-site restaurants where you can enjoy wine and food pairings. You can savor gourmet meals or light snacks that complement the wines.

Live Events: Depending on the winery's schedule, you might encounter live events, such as live music performances, art exhibitions, or wine-themed festivals. These events add to the festive atmosphere.

Winery Shops: Wineries often have gift shops or wine boutiques where you can purchase bottles of wine, wine-related accessories, and local artisan products. It's an opportunity to take home some of your favorite wines.

Accessibility: Wineries generally aim to provide accessibility for all visitors, including those with disabilities. Inquire about specific accommodations you may need.

Reservations: Some wineries may require reservations for tours and tastings, especially during busy seasons. It's a good idea to plan ahead and check with the wineries you plan to visit.

Designated Drivers: If you plan to indulge in wine tastings, it's advisable to have a designated driver or arrange for transportation to ensure a safe journey home.

Scenic Drives: The wine regions of Ohio often offer scenic routes and byways that connect various wineries. Plan your tour to enjoy leisurely drives through the countryside.

Local Events: Check the local events calendar for wine festivals and special events happening in Ohio's wine regions. These events can be a great way to experience the local wine culture.

Ohio's wine country is known for its welcoming wineries, award-winning wines, and genuine hospitality. Whether you're a wine enthusiast, a food lover, or simply seeking a relaxing and scenic getaway, a wine tour of Ohio's wine country offers a memorable and enjoyable experience for wine lovers and travelers of all backgrounds.

84. Visit the Playhouse Square chandelier.

Visiting the Playhouse Square chandelier in Cleveland is an opportunity to experience a dazzling and iconic piece of public art. Here's what you can expect when you visit the Playhouse Square chandelier:

Location: The Playhouse Square chandelier is typically located in the heart of downtown Cleveland, often suspended above the intersection of Euclid Avenue and East 14th Street. It's a prominent and easily accessible landmark in the city.

Travel to Cleveland Ohio

Dazzling Design: The chandelier is a stunning work of art and engineering, featuring thousands of crystals that catch the light and create a mesmerizing display. It's a symbol of elegance and grandeur.

Impressive Size: The Playhouse Square chandelier is known for its impressive size, often measuring several stories in height. Its sheer scale adds to its visual impact and makes it a must-see attraction.

Interactive Lighting: In many cases, the chandelier is equipped with interactive lighting features that allow for color changes and dynamic lighting displays. The lighting can be adjusted to create different moods and atmospheres, particularly during special events and occasions.

Local Landmark: The chandelier has become a beloved local landmark and a symbol of the revitalization of Playhouse Square, one of the largest performing arts districts in the United States. It's often featured in photographs and serves as a meeting point for locals and visitors.

Accessibility: The chandelier is typically easy to access, and you can view it from the surrounding sidewalks and plazas. Be sure to check if there are any guided tours or events that provide additional insights into the chandelier's history and design.

Photography: The chandelier's striking design and lighting effects make it a popular subject for photography. Capture its beauty and share your photos with friends and family.

Special Events: Playhouse Square often hosts special events and performances in the area around the chandelier. Check the Playhouse Square website or local event listings for any upcoming shows or gatherings that coincide with your visit.

Local Dining and Entertainment: The Playhouse Square district is home to a variety of restaurants, bars, theaters, and entertainment venues. Consider dining at one of the local restaurants or catching a live performance while you're in the area.

Hours: While the chandelier itself is always visible, the surrounding district may have different operating hours depending on the day and specific events. Check ahead of time to plan your visit accordingly.

Visiting the Playhouse Square chandelier is a chance to appreciate the intersection of art, architecture, and urban revitalization. Whether you're a fan of public art, interested in the local culture, or simply looking to admire a captivating piece of design, the chandelier is a must-see attraction in Cleveland.

85. Attend the Great Lakes Burning River Fest.

Attending the Great Lakes Burning River Fest in Cleveland is a fun and environmentally conscious way to enjoy live music, craft beer, and local food while supporting initiatives to protect and restore the Great Lakes. Here's what you can expect when you attend this festival:

Location: The Great Lakes Burning River Fest is typically held at a scenic waterfront location in Cleveland, often along the Cuyahoga River or Lake Erie shoreline. The choice of venue adds to the festival's natural beauty and ambiance.

Live Music: The festival features live music performances by local and regional bands and musicians. You can enjoy a variety of musical genres, from rock and folk to blues and indie. Check the festival's lineup to see which acts will be performing during your visit.

Craft Beer: One of the highlights of the festival is the craft beer selection. You can sample a wide range of craft brews from local and regional breweries. Some festivals may feature special beer releases or collaborations unique to the event.

Local Food: Savor delicious dishes from local food vendors and food trucks. The festival often showcases Cleveland's culinary scene, offering a diverse array of food options to complement your beer tasting.

Environmental Focus: The Burning River Fest is known for its environmental advocacy. It raises awareness about the importance of preserving the Great Lakes and the Cuyahoga River, which famously caught fire in 1969, leading to significant environmental reforms. Expect educational exhibits and information about local environmental organizations.

Sustainable Practices: The festival typically incorporates sustainable practices, such as waste reduction, recycling, and eco-friendly initiatives. It's an opportunity to learn about eco-conscious choices and practices.

Art and Activism: You may encounter art installations, exhibits, and interactive displays that explore environmental themes and encourage active participation in sustainability efforts.

Family-Friendly Activities: Some festivals offer family-friendly activities, such as children's entertainment, games, and educational programs related to environmental conservation.

Local Craft Vendors: Explore booths and stalls featuring local artisans, crafters, and eco-friendly products. It's a chance to support local businesses and find unique, sustainable goods.

Accessibility: Festival organizers often aim to provide accessibility for all attendees, including those with disabilities. Inquire about specific accommodations you may need.

Dates and Tickets: Check the Great Lakes Burning River Fest's official website or local event listings for information on festival dates, ticket prices, and any special promotions or packages.

Attending the Great Lakes Burning River Fest is not only a fantastic way to enjoy live music, craft beer, and local food but also an opportunity to contribute to environmental causes and learn about the importance of preserving the Great Lakes region. Whether you're an environmental advocate, a music enthusiast, or simply looking for a great time, this festival offers a unique and impactful experience.

86. Explore the Irish Cultural Garden.

Exploring the Irish Cultural Garden in Cleveland offers a serene and culturally enriching experience, celebrating the heritage and contributions of the Irish community. Here's what you can expect when you visit this beautiful garden:

Location: The Irish Cultural Garden is typically situated within the Cleveland Cultural Gardens, a collection of ethnic gardens along Martin Luther King Jr. Drive in Rockefeller Park. It's easily accessible and part of a larger cultural and scenic area.

Garden Design: The Irish Cultural Garden showcases traditional Irish design elements, often featuring pathways, stone walls, and lush greenery that reflect the landscapes of Ireland. It's a serene and inviting space for visitors.

Statues and Monuments: The garden may contain statues and monuments that pay tribute to notable Irish figures, historical events, and cultural symbols. These sculptures serve as focal points and provide educational insights.

Plantings: The garden's plantings typically include native Irish plants and flowers, such as shamrocks, heather, and Irish moss, creating an authentic atmosphere reminiscent of Ireland's countryside.

Educational Signage: Look for informative signage and plaques that provide details about Irish culture, history, and the contributions of the Irish diaspora to Cleveland and the United States. You can learn about famous Irish Americans and their impact.

Photography: The picturesque setting of the Irish Cultural Garden makes it an ideal location for photography. Capture the beauty of the garden, statues, and natural surroundings during your visit.

Cultural Events: Depending on the time of year, the Irish Cultural Garden may host cultural events, festivals, or performances that celebrate Irish heritage through music, dance, and other artistic expressions. Check local event listings for any upcoming activities.

Accessibility: The garden is typically designed to be accessible to all visitors, including those with disabilities. Inquire about specific accommodations you may need.

Community Engagement: The Irish Cultural Garden often serves as a hub for the local Irish community, fostering connections and promoting cultural awareness. Consider reaching out to local Irish organizations or cultural groups for additional insights and involvement.

Hours: Check the Cleveland Cultural Gardens' official website or local listings for the Irish Cultural Garden's hours of operation, seasonal variations, and any special events.

Travel to Cleveland Ohio

Visiting the Irish Cultural Garden provides a peaceful and educational experience where you can appreciate the beauty of Irish culture and heritage. Whether you have Irish roots or simply have an interest in world cultures, this garden offers a tranquil and enriching visit within the context of the larger Cleveland Cultural Gardens.

87. Take a pottery or ceramics class at the Cleveland Institute of Art.

Participating in a pottery or ceramics class at the Cleveland Institute of Art (CIA) is an excellent way to explore your creativity and develop your skills in working with clay. Here's what you can expect when you enroll in a pottery or ceramics class at CIA:

Course Offerings: The Cleveland Institute of Art typically offers a range of pottery and ceramics courses for students of all skill levels, from beginners to advanced artists. These courses may cover handbuilding techniques, wheel throwing, glazing, and firing.

Experienced Instructors: Classes are often taught by experienced and talented instructors who can provide expert guidance and feedback on your work. They may offer demonstrations, one-on-one instruction, and critiques to help you improve your pottery and ceramics skills.

Studio Facilities: CIA usually provides well-equipped studio facilities with access to pottery wheels, kilns, clay, glazes, and various tools and equipment. You'll have the opportunity to work in a creative and inspiring environment.

Projects and Assignments: During the course, you'll typically complete a series of projects and assignments that allow you to explore different techniques and styles in pottery and ceramics. These projects may include creating functional pottery, sculptural pieces, and decorative items.

Materials: Course fees often include basic materials such as clay and glazes, but students may need to purchase additional supplies or specialized materials as they progress in their studies.

Critiques and Feedback: Instructors and peers often provide constructive feedback and critiques during class, helping you refine your artistic vision and technical skills. This collaborative learning environment can be both motivating and instructive.

Community: Enrolling in a class at CIA means you'll become part of a creative community of artists and students who share your passion for pottery and ceramics. You can exchange ideas, learn from your peers, and build valuable connections.

Exhibitions and Events: The Cleveland Institute of Art frequently hosts exhibitions and events showcasing the work of students and faculty. This provides opportunities for you to display your creations and gain exposure as an emerging artist.

Registration: Check the Cleveland Institute of Art's official website or contact the institution for information on course offerings, registration details, tuition fees, and any prerequisites or portfolio requirements.

Whether you're a beginner looking to explore pottery and ceramics as a hobby or an experienced artist seeking to further your skills and knowledge, taking a class at the Cleveland Institute of Art can be a rewarding and creative endeavor. It's a chance to immerse yourself in the world of ceramics, express your artistic vision, and create beautiful and functional pieces of art.

88.Attend the Cleveland Tall Ships Festival.

Attending the Cleveland Tall Ships Festival is a captivating and maritime-themed experience that allows you to explore historic sailing vessels, learn about maritime heritage, and enjoy a range of activities. Here's what you can expect when you attend this festival:

Historic Tall Ships: The festival typically features a fleet of majestic tall ships, some of which are replicas of historic vessels from the Age of Sail. You can explore these magnificent ships up close, marvel at their intricate rigging and sails, and learn about their history and significance.

Ship Tours: Many of the tall ships offer guided tours conducted by knowledgeable crew members. These tours provide insights into the ship's design, construction, navigation, and daily life on board during their heyday.

Travel to Cleveland Ohio

Sailing Excursions: Some festivals offer the opportunity to go on sailing excursions on the tall ships. You can experience the thrill of sailing on these beautiful vessels and even lend a hand with the crew's tasks, such as raising sails or steering.

Maritime History: Explore exhibits and displays that delve into maritime history, including the role of tall ships in trade, exploration, and naval warfare. You can learn about the challenges and adventures faced by sailors of the past.

Nautical Arts and Crafts: The festival often features nautical-themed arts and crafts vendors, where you can find maritime-inspired artwork, jewelry, clothing, and souvenirs.

Entertainment: Enjoy live music, maritime-themed performances, and entertainment suitable for visitors of all ages. These activities add to the festival's festive atmosphere.

Food and Beverage: Savor delicious food and beverages from local vendors and food trucks. You can sample regional cuisine and enjoy a meal with a view of the ships.

Children's Activities: Festivals frequently offer family-friendly activities such as children's games, face painting, and educational programs that introduce young visitors to maritime history and science.

Accessibility: Organizers typically aim to provide accessibility for all attendees, including those with disabilities. Inquire about specific accommodations you may need.

Photography: The tall ships, with their stunning sails and maritime charm, make for excellent photography subjects. Capture the beauty of these vessels against the backdrop of the water.

Dates and Tickets: Check the official website of the Cleveland Tall Ships Festival or local event listings for information on festival dates, ticket prices, and any special events or programs.

Attending the Cleveland Tall Ships Festival is a chance to step back in time, immerse yourself in maritime history, and experience the allure of tall ships. Whether you're a history buff, a sailing enthusiast, or simply seeking a unique and memorable event, this festival offers a captivating and educational maritime adventure.

89. Visit the Greater Cleveland Film Commission.

Visiting the Greater Cleveland Film Commission (GCFC) offers insights into the film and media industry in the region and provides an opportunity to learn about the organization's efforts to promote filmmaking in Cleveland. Here's what you can expect when you visit the GCFC:

Location: The Greater Cleveland Film Commission is typically located in Cleveland, often in a central or easily accessible area. Check the organization's official website or contact them for their current address and visiting hours.

Mission and Purpose: Upon your visit, you can learn about the GCFC's mission, objectives, and the role it plays in supporting the local film and media industry. The organization often advocates for Cleveland as a filming location and assists filmmakers with resources and incentives.

Educational Programs: The GCFC may offer educational programs, workshops, and seminars related to filmmaking, media production, and the entertainment industry. These programs can provide valuable insights for aspiring filmmakers and industry professionals.

Local Filmmaking Resources: Explore the resources and services that the GCFC offers to filmmakers, including information on permits, locations, talent, crew, and equipment available in the Cleveland area.

Community Engagement: The GCFC often engages with the local community and may participate in events, film festivals, and initiatives that promote film and media culture. They may also collaborate with local schools and universities to support film education.

Film and TV Productions: Learn about recent and upcoming film and TV productions that have chosen Cleveland as a filming location. The GCFC can provide information about how these projects contribute to the local economy and creative scene.

Travel to Cleveland Ohio

Advocacy and Networking: Discover how the GCFC advocates for the growth of the local film and media industry and fosters connections between filmmakers, industry professionals, and local businesses.

Accessibility: The GCFC typically aims to provide accessibility for all visitors, including those with disabilities. Inquire about specific accommodations you may need.

Publications and Resources: The organization may offer publications, resources, and materials related to the film industry and its impact on the Cleveland community. These resources can be informative for visitors interested in the local film scene.

Membership Opportunities: If you have a strong interest in supporting the GCFC's mission and becoming involved in the local film community, inquire about membership opportunities and how you can contribute.

Events and Fundraisers: Keep an eye out for events, fundraisers, and special screenings hosted by the GCFC. These events can be a great way to engage with fellow film enthusiasts and support the organization's initiatives.

Visiting the Greater Cleveland Film Commission provides an opportunity to gain a deeper understanding of the film and media industry's presence in Cleveland and the organization's efforts to promote and support it. Whether you're a filmmaker, a film enthusiast, or simply curious about the role of film commissions in shaping a city's creative landscape, a visit to the GCFC can be an informative and inspiring experience.

90. Explore the Arabic Cultural Garden.

Exploring the Arabic Cultural Garden in Cleveland allows you to immerse yourself in the rich heritage and artistic expressions of the Arabic-speaking world. Here's what you can expect when you visit this cultural garden:

Location: The Arabic Cultural Garden is typically located within the Cleveland Cultural Gardens, a collection of ethnic gardens along Martin Luther King Jr. Drive in Rockefeller Park. It's easily accessible and part of a larger cultural and scenic area.

Garden Design: The Arabic Cultural Garden often features elements of traditional Arabic design, including intricate tilework, geometric patterns, and lush greenery. It's designed to evoke the beauty and tranquility of Arabic gardens.

Statues and Monuments: The garden may contain statues, sculptures, and monuments that pay homage to prominent figures, historical events, and cultural symbols from Arabic-speaking countries. These artworks serve as focal points and provide educational insights.

Plants and Floral Displays: The garden's plantings typically include a selection of plants and flowers commonly found in Arabic gardens, creating a serene and aromatic atmosphere.

Educational Signage: Look for informative signage and plaques that provide details about Arabic culture, history, and the contributions of Arabic-speaking communities to Cleveland and the United States. You can learn about notable Arab Americans and their impact.

Photography: The picturesque setting of the Arabic Cultural Garden makes it an ideal location for photography. Capture the beauty of the garden, sculptures, and natural surroundings during your visit.

Cultural Events: Depending on the time of year, the garden may host cultural events, festivals, or performances that celebrate Arabic culture through music, dance, literature, and other artistic expressions. Check local event listings for any upcoming activities.

Community Engagement: The Arabic Cultural Garden often serves as a gathering place for the local Arabic-speaking community, fostering connections and promoting cultural awareness. Consider reaching out to local Arabic cultural organizations or community groups for additional insights and involvement.

Accessibility: The garden is typically designed to be accessible to all visitors, including those with disabilities. Inquire about specific accommodations you may need.

Hours: Check the Cleveland Cultural Gardens' official website or local listings for the Arabic Cultural Garden's hours of operation, seasonal variations, and any special events.

Visiting the Arabic Cultural Garden offers a peaceful and educational experience where you can appreciate the beauty of Arabic culture and heritage.

Travel to Cleveland Ohio

Whether you have Arabic roots, an interest in world cultures, or a love for garden aesthetics, this garden provides a serene and enriching visit within the context of the larger Cleveland Cultural Gardens.

91. Go sailing on Lake Erie.

Sailing on Lake Erie is a delightful experience that allows you to enjoy the natural beauty and recreational opportunities offered by one of the Great Lakes. Here's what you can expect when you go sailing on Lake Erie:

Charter Services: Lake Erie is home to various charter services and sailing clubs that offer sailing excursions for individuals, couples, families, and groups. You can typically choose from different types of sailing experiences, including private charters, group tours, and lessons.

Experienced Captains: Many charter services provide experienced captains and crews who are knowledgeable about Lake Erie's waters. They prioritize safety and ensure a smooth and enjoyable sailing experience.

Types of Sailboats: Depending on the charter service, you may have the opportunity to sail on various types of sailboats, such as sloops, catamarans, and schooners. The choice of sailboat can influence your experience, from leisurely cruising to more exhilarating rides.

Scenic Views: Sailing on Lake Erie offers stunning views of the lake's shores, including picturesque landscapes, beaches, lighthouses, and waterfront communities. The sight of the open water and the horizon can be incredibly peaceful and awe-inspiring.

Wildlife and Nature: Lake Erie is known for its diverse wildlife and bird populations. While sailing, you may spot various bird species, including seagulls and eagles, as well as the occasional glimpse of fish or marine life.

Sunsets and Sunrises: Lake Erie is renowned for its beautiful sunsets and sunrises. Sailing during these times can provide a memorable and romantic experience as you watch the sky transform with vibrant colors.

Sailing Lessons: If you're new to sailing or looking to improve your sailing skills, some charter services offer sailing lessons. Certified instructors can teach you the basics of sailing, navigation, and safety.

Accessibility: Charter services typically aim to provide accessibility for all passengers, including those with disabilities. Inquire about specific accommodations you may need.

Duration and Packages: Charter services may offer different sailing packages, including half-day, full-day, and sunset cruises. Some packages may include amenities like meals, snacks, and beverages.

Reservations: It's advisable to make reservations in advance, especially during peak sailing seasons. Check with the charter service for availability and booking procedures.

Weather Considerations: Keep in mind that weather conditions on Lake Erie can change quickly. Charter services prioritize safety and may need to reschedule or cancel trips if weather conditions become unfavorable.

Sailing on Lake Erie offers a unique and peaceful way to connect with nature, explore the lake's waters, and enjoy a relaxing day on the water. Whether you're an experienced sailor or a novice looking to try something new, a sailing excursion on Lake Erie can be a memorable and enjoyable adventure.

92. Attend the Cleveland Whiskey Festival.

Attending the Cleveland Whiskey Festival is a wonderful way to explore the world of whiskey, sample a wide range of whiskey brands and expressions, and gain a deeper appreciation for this popular spirit. Here's what you can expect when you attend this festival:

Location: The Cleveland Whiskey Festival is typically held at a central venue in Cleveland. Check the festival's official website or local event listings for the specific location and details.

Whiskey Tastings: The festival features an extensive selection of whiskey brands, including Scotch, bourbon, Irish whiskey, rye, and more. Attendees have the opportunity to participate in tastings, where you can sample various whiskeys and learn about their flavors, aromas, and production methods.

Whiskey Experts: Knowledgeable whiskey experts and brand ambassadors are often present to provide insights into the whiskeys being showcased. They can

Travel to Cleveland Ohio

offer information about the distillation process, aging, and the unique characteristics of each whiskey.

Food Pairings: Many whiskey festivals incorporate food pairings that complement the flavors of the whiskey. You can expect to enjoy gourmet dishes or snacks that enhance the tasting experience.

Cocktail Demonstrations: Some festivals feature cocktail demonstrations and mixology workshops where you can learn how to craft whiskey-based cocktails. It's an opportunity to discover new cocktail recipes and techniques.

Educational Seminars: Look for educational seminars and workshops that delve into the history of whiskey, its production, and regional variations. These sessions can deepen your knowledge of whiskey.

Vendor Booths: Whiskey-related vendors and exhibitors may set up booths, offering products like whiskey accessories, glassware, books, and even bottles for purchase.

Live Entertainment: Festivals often include live music, entertainment, or cultural performances to create a lively and enjoyable atmosphere.

Networking: Whiskey enthusiasts, industry professionals, and fellow attendees provide a great opportunity for networking and sharing your passion for whiskey.

Designated Drivers: If you plan to participate in whiskey tastings, consider arranging for a designated driver or alternative transportation to ensure a safe journey home.

Ticket Information: Check the festival's official website or local event listings for ticket prices, package options, and any special promotions or VIP experiences.

Responsible Tasting: Whiskey festivals typically encourage responsible drinking. Be mindful of your alcohol consumption and pace yourself during tastings.

Attending the Cleveland Whiskey Festival is a fantastic way to expand your palate, discover new whiskey brands, and enjoy a social and cultural experience centered around this beloved spirit. Whether you're a whiskey connoisseur or someone looking to explore the world of whiskey, this festival offers a memorable and flavorful adventure.

93. Visit the Cleveland Firefighters Memorial.

Visiting the Cleveland Firefighters Memorial is a way to pay tribute to the brave firefighters who have served the city of Cleveland and to honor their dedication and sacrifice. Here's what you can expect when you visit this memorial:

Location: The Cleveland Firefighters Memorial is typically located at a prominent location in the city, often near a fire station or within a park. Check the memorial's official location and any visitor information to plan your visit.

Memorial Design: The memorial is designed to commemorate the heroic efforts of firefighters. It may include sculptures, plaques, inscriptions, and architectural elements that symbolize the courage and sacrifice of firefighters.

Dedication: Many fire department memorials feature inscriptions or dedications that honor firefighters who have lost their lives in the line of duty. Take a moment to read these tributes and reflect on their significance.

Sculptures: Firefighters memorials often include sculptures depicting firefighters in action. These sculptures capture the bravery and selflessness of firefighters as they respond to emergencies.

Reflection and Remembrance: The memorial provides a peaceful space for reflection and remembrance. Visitors can pay their respects, express gratitude for the service of firefighters, and remember those who have made the ultimate sacrifice.

Photography: The memorial's design and sculptures make it a meaningful and picturesque location for photography. Consider taking photographs to document your visit and to share the significance of the memorial with others.

Accessibility: Memorials are typically designed to be accessible to all visitors, including those with disabilities. Inquire about specific accommodations you may need.

Travel to Cleveland Ohio

Local Fire Department: You may find that the memorial is located near a local fire station. If you're interested in learning more about the history and current operations of the fire department, consider stopping by the nearby station or contacting them in advance to arrange a visit.

Community Events: Some memorials host community events, ceremonies, or annual commemorations to honor firefighters and their families. Check local event listings to see if there are any upcoming events associated with the memorial.

Educational Opportunities: Memorials often offer educational opportunities for visitors to learn about the history of firefighting, fire safety, and the role of firefighters in the community. Look for informational displays or resources.

Visiting the Cleveland Firefighters Memorial is a meaningful way to show appreciation for the dedication and sacrifices of firefighters who serve the community. It's a place of reflection, honor, and gratitude, where you can pay tribute to the heroes who protect lives and property in times of emergency.

94. Explore the Shakespeare Garden.

Exploring the Shakespeare Garden in Cleveland is a delightful experience for lovers of literature and botany alike. Here's what you can expect when you visit this charming garden:

Location: The Shakespeare Garden is typically located within the Cleveland Cultural Gardens, a collection of ethnic gardens along Martin Luther King Jr. Drive in Rockefeller Park. It's easily accessible and part of a larger cultural and scenic area.

Garden Design: The Shakespeare Garden is designed to pay homage to the renowned English playwright William Shakespeare. It often features elements reminiscent of English cottage gardens, including a variety of herbs, flowers, and plants mentioned in Shakespeare's works.

Botanical Collections: The garden is planted with a diverse selection of plants and flowers that are mentioned in Shakespeare's plays and sonnets. Each plant is typically labeled with quotes from Shakespeare's works, connecting the literature to the botanical world.

Educational Signage: Look for informative signage and plaques that provide details about Shakespeare's life and works, as well as explanations of the plants and their relevance to his writings. This adds an educational dimension to your visit.

Statues and Monuments: The garden may contain statues, sculptures, and monuments dedicated to William Shakespeare and his literary contributions. These artistic features serve as focal points within the garden.

Scenic Setting: The picturesque setting of the Shakespeare Garden, with its colorful blooms and aromatic herbs, makes it an ideal location for leisurely strolls, picnics, and relaxation. It's a serene oasis within the city.

Photography: The garden's beauty and literary connections make it a popular spot for photography. Capture the vibrant colors, fragrant blossoms, and Shakespearean quotes during your visit.

Cultural Events: Depending on the time of year, the Shakespeare Garden may host cultural events, literary readings, or performances related to Shakespeare's works. Check local event listings for any upcoming activities.

Accessibility: The garden is typically designed to be accessible to all visitors, including those with disabilities. Inquire about specific accommodations you may need.

Community Engagement: The Shakespeare Garden often serves as a gathering place for local literature enthusiasts and fans of Shakespeare's works. Consider reaching out to local literary organizations or theater groups for additional insights and involvement.

Hours: Check the Cleveland Cultural Gardens' official website or local listings for the Shakespeare Garden's hours of operation, seasonal variations, and any special events.

Visiting the Shakespeare Garden provides a tranquil and educational experience where you can appreciate the beauty of nature and the enduring influence of one of the world's greatest playwrights. Whether you have a deep appreciation for Shakespearean literature or simply enjoy the serenity of well-tended gardens, this cultural oasis offers a peaceful and enriching visit within the context of the larger Cleveland Cultural Gardens.

Travel to Cleveland Ohio

95. Attend the Brite Winter Festival.

Attending the Brite Winter Festival is a vibrant and immersive experience that celebrates music, art, and community spirit in the heart of winter. Here's what you can expect when you attend this festival:

Location: The Brite Winter Festival is typically held in various venues throughout Cleveland, often in the Ohio City neighborhood. Check the festival's official website or local event listings for the specific locations and details.

Winter Wonderland: As a winter festival, Brite Winter embraces the season and the snowy landscape. Expect to enjoy winter-themed decorations, snow sculptures, and a cozy atmosphere, making it a unique and memorable experience.

Live Music: The festival features a diverse lineup of live music performances across multiple stages and venues. You can expect to hear a wide range of music genres, from indie rock and folk to electronic and experimental. Local and national acts often grace the festival's stages.

Art Installations: Brite Winter often incorporates art installations and interactive art experiences that engage attendees and add an element of creativity to the festival. These installations can be visually captivating and thought-provoking.

Food and Drink: Local food vendors and food trucks typically offer a variety of culinary delights to satisfy your appetite. You can sample regional cuisine, street food, and delicious winter-themed treats. Don't forget to explore the local craft beer and beverage scene.

Interactive Activities: The festival often includes interactive activities and games that encourage attendees to participate and have fun. Look for activities like ice sculpting, winter sports, or themed photo booths.

Community Engagement: Brite Winter is known for fostering a strong sense of community. You can connect with fellow festival-goers, artists, and local organizations, all while enjoying the winter festivities.

Local Artisans: Browse through artisan vendor booths to discover unique and handmade crafts, artworks, and merchandise. It's an excellent opportunity to support local artists and find one-of-a-kind souvenirs.

People Who Know Publishing

Family-Friendly: While Brite Winter is known for its vibrant nightlife, there are often family-friendly activities and programming during the daytime hours. Families can enjoy music, art, and winter fun together.

Accessibility: Festival organizers typically aim to provide accessibility for all attendees, including those with disabilities. Inquire about specific accommodations you may need.

Tickets: Check the festival's official website or local event listings for ticket prices, package options, and any special promotions or VIP experiences. Some events may be ticketed, while others are free to attend.

Weather Considerations: Be prepared for winter weather. Dress warmly, wear appropriate footwear, and consider bringing hand warmers and other cold-weather essentials.

Attending the Brite Winter Festival offers a unique way to embrace the winter season, enjoy live music and art, and celebrate the sense of community in Cleveland. Whether you're a music enthusiast, an art lover, or simply looking for a winter adventure, this festival provides a memorable and dynamic experience that showcases the city's creative spirit.

96. Take a ride on the Lolly the Trolley tour.

Taking a ride on Lolly the Trolley tour in Cleveland is a fun and informative way to explore the city's landmarks, history, and culture. Here's what you can expect when you embark on a Lolly the Trolley tour:

Trolley Experience: Lolly the Trolley is a charming and iconic mode of transportation in Cleveland. The trolley itself is often a vintage-style vehicle with character, and the tours are conducted by knowledgeable guides who provide entertaining and educational commentary throughout the journey.

Scenic Routes: Lolly the Trolley tours typically offer various routes that cover different parts of Cleveland. You can choose a tour that focuses on downtown attractions, historic neighborhoods, or specific themes, depending on your interests.

Travel to Cleveland Ohio

Historical Insights: The tour guides are well-versed in Cleveland's history, architecture, and notable landmarks. They share interesting stories and historical facts about the city, giving you a deeper appreciation for its rich heritage.

Landmarks and Points of Interest: The tours often include stops at key landmarks and points of interest in Cleveland. You'll have the opportunity to disembark, take photos, and explore these sites up close before reboarding the trolley.

Comfort and Convenience: Lolly the Trolley tours provide a comfortable and convenient way to see the city. The trolley is heated in the winter and air-conditioned in the summer, ensuring a pleasant ride regardless of the season.

Audio Enhancement: Some tours offer audio enhancement systems, allowing all passengers to hear the guide's commentary clearly. This is especially useful if you're seated farther away from the guide.

Specialty Tours: Depending on the tour company and the time of year, you may find specialty tours related to holidays, seasonal events, or specific themes. Check with the tour operator for any unique offerings during your visit.

Accessibility: Lolly the Trolley tours typically aim to provide accessibility for all passengers, including those with disabilities. Inquire about specific accommodations you may need.

Tickets and Reservations: Check the official website of Lolly the Trolley or contact them directly for information on tour schedules, ticket prices, and reservations. It's advisable to book your tickets in advance, especially during peak tourist seasons.

Duration: Tour durations vary depending on the specific route and stops, so be sure to check the details when making your plans.

Group Tours: Lolly the Trolley tours are suitable for individuals, couples, families, and groups. Private group tours can often be arranged for special occasions or corporate events.

A ride on Lolly the Trolley offers a relaxed and informative way to explore Cleveland's diverse neighborhoods, historical sites, and vibrant culture. Whether you're a visitor looking to discover the city or a local wanting to learn more about your hometown, a Lolly the Trolley tour can be an enjoyable and enlightening experience.

97. Visit the "Free Stamp" sculpture.

Visiting the "Free Stamp" sculpture in Cleveland is an opportunity to appreciate a unique and iconic piece of public art. Here's what you can expect when you visit this distinctive sculpture:

Location: The "Free Stamp" sculpture is located in downtown Cleveland, typically situated in Willard Park. It's centrally located and easily accessible, making it a convenient stop during your exploration of the city.

Sculpture Design: The "Free Stamp" sculpture is a large and eye-catching artwork created by world-renowned artist Claes Oldenburg and his wife, Coosje van Bruggen. It resembles a gigantic rubber stamp with the word "FREE" on its face. The sculpture challenges traditional ideas of art and objects by enlarging an everyday item to monumental proportions.

Interpretation: The sculpture's meaning is open to interpretation, but it's often seen as a symbol of freedom of expression and the idea that art should be "free" from constraints and boundaries. It's also a playful commentary on the function of a rubber stamp, which typically marks documents with approval or authority.

Photography: The "Free Stamp" sculpture is a popular spot for photography, both for its artistic value and its unusual size. Visitors often take photos of themselves or their friends interacting with the sculpture, such as pretending to stamp something with it.

Surrounding Area: Willard Park, where the sculpture is located, provides a green and pleasant space to relax and enjoy the outdoors. You can take a leisurely stroll around the park or have a picnic nearby.

Accessibility: The sculpture and the surrounding area are typically designed to be accessible to all visitors, including those with disabilities.

Public Art: The "Free Stamp" sculpture is a prime example of public art in Cleveland, and it's emblematic of the city's commitment to promoting art and culture in public spaces.

Travel to Cleveland Ohio

Visitor Center: Depending on the time of your visit, you may find a visitor center or information booth nearby where you can gather additional information about the sculpture and other attractions in the area.

Art and Culture: Cleveland is home to a thriving arts and culture scene, and the "Free Stamp" sculpture is just one of many artistic treasures you can explore while in the city. Consider checking out local galleries, museums, and theaters during your visit.

A visit to the "Free Stamp" sculpture provides an opportunity to engage with a thought-provoking work of art that challenges conventional notions of scale and meaning. Whether you're an art enthusiast or simply curious about unique public art installations, the "Free Stamp" is a fascinating addition to your exploration of Cleveland's cultural landscape.

98. Attend the Cleveland Asian Lantern Festival.

Attending the Cleveland Asian Lantern Festival is a captivating and cultural experience that celebrates the beauty of Asian art, traditions, and illuminated lantern displays. Here's what you can expect when you attend this vibrant festival:

Location: The Cleveland Asian Lantern Festival is typically held in a scenic outdoor setting, often at Cleveland Metroparks Zoo or another suitable venue. Check the festival's official website or local event listings for the specific location and details.

Lantern Displays: The festival is known for its stunning lantern displays, which feature intricate and colorful lanterns in various shapes and sizes. These lanterns may depict animals, mythological creatures, traditional symbols, and scenes from Asian culture and folklore.

Illumination: The lantern displays come to life after sunset, as they are beautifully illuminated with LED lights, creating a magical and enchanting atmosphere. The festival is especially captivating in the evening.

Cultural Performances: Attendees can enjoy a diverse lineup of cultural performances that showcase Asian arts, music, dance, and traditions. These performances often feature talented artists from both local and international communities.

Food and Beverages: The festival typically offers a wide array of Asian cuisine and beverages, allowing you to sample delicious dishes and treats from various Asian cultures. Explore different flavors, from sushi and dumplings to Thai curry and bubble tea.

Arts and Crafts: Browse through artisan stalls and craft booths where you can discover Asian-inspired artwork, crafts, jewelry, clothing, and unique souvenirs. It's an excellent opportunity to support local artisans and find distinctive items.

Interactive Activities: Some festivals include interactive activities for attendees, such as lantern-making workshops, calligraphy demonstrations, or traditional tea ceremonies. These activities offer hands-on cultural experiences.

Family-Friendly: The Cleveland Asian Lantern Festival is often family-friendly, with activities and entertainment suitable for all ages. Children can enjoy the lantern displays and participate in kid-friendly activities.

Photography: The festival's illuminated lantern displays create a visually stunning backdrop for photography. Be sure to bring your camera or smartphone to capture the colorful and artistic lanterns.

Accessibility: Festival organizers typically aim to provide accessibility for all attendees, including those with disabilities. Inquire about specific accommodations you may need.

Tickets: Check the festival's official website or local event listings for ticket prices, package options, and any special promotions. Some events may be ticketed, while others are free to attend.

Event Dates: The Cleveland Asian Lantern Festival is often held during specific dates or seasons, so be sure to check the festival's schedule and plan your visit accordingly.

Attending the Cleveland Asian Lantern Festival offers a unique opportunity to immerse yourself in the beauty, artistry, and culture of Asia. Whether you have a deep appreciation for Asian traditions or simply want to experience a dazzling and multicultural event, this festival provides an enchanting and memorable evening of cultural celebration.

Travel to Cleveland Ohio

99. Explore the Ariel Pearl Center.

Exploring the Ariel Pearl Center in Cleveland is an opportunity to discover a unique and versatile event venue with historical charm. Here's what you can expect when you visit or explore this distinctive space:

Location: The Ariel Pearl Center is typically situated in the heart of Cleveland or a convenient downtown location. Check the venue's official website or contact them directly for specific location details and directions.

Historical Venue: The Ariel Pearl Center is often housed within a historic building, adding character and ambiance to your visit. The architecture and design may reflect the building's rich history, providing a charming backdrop for various events.

Event Space: The venue is primarily known as a space for hosting a wide range of events, including weddings, corporate gatherings, galas, parties, and more. Explore the different event spaces within the Ariel Pearl Center, which may include ballrooms, banquet halls, outdoor patios, and more.

Interior Design: The interior of the Ariel Pearl Center is typically designed with attention to detail, featuring elegant decor, chandeliers, and architectural elements that contribute to a refined and inviting atmosphere.

Private Events: Depending on the time of your visit, you may find the Ariel Pearl Center set up for a private event. While touring the space, you can appreciate how it transforms to accommodate various occasions.

Weddings: The Ariel Pearl Center is a popular choice for wedding ceremonies and receptions. If you're planning a wedding, consider scheduling a visit to see how the venue can be customized to suit your preferences and style.

Corporate Functions: The venue is also suitable for corporate events, meetings, conferences, and other business-related gatherings. You can inquire about available amenities and services for corporate clients.

Social Events: Social events such as galas, fundraisers, and parties are often hosted at the Ariel Pearl Center. These events may feature live entertainment, dining, and a festive atmosphere.

Catering Services: Some events at the Ariel Pearl Center offer catering services with a variety of menu options to suit different tastes and preferences. Explore the catering offerings if you attend an event that includes dining.

Accessibility: The Ariel Pearl Center typically aims to provide accessibility for all visitors and event attendees, including those with disabilities. Inquire about specific accommodations you may need.

Event Calendar: Check the Ariel Pearl Center's official website or event listings for information on upcoming events, open houses, or tours that may be available to the public.

Whether you're planning an event, considering a wedding venue, or simply curious about the Ariel Pearl Center's historical and architectural appeal, a visit or exploration of this versatile venue can provide valuable insights into its potential for hosting memorable occasions in Cleveland.

100. Go on a Cleveland Brewery Tour.

Going on a Cleveland brewery tour is a fantastic way to explore the city's thriving craft beer scene, sample a variety of local brews, and learn about the brewing process. Here's what you can expect when you embark on a brewery tour in Cleveland:

Brewery Hopping: Cleveland boasts a diverse array of breweries, ranging from small craft breweries to larger, well-established ones. Your brewery tour will typically involve visiting multiple breweries in one day.

Beer Tastings: At each brewery you visit, you'll have the opportunity to taste a selection of their beers. Most tours include flights or samples of their flagship and seasonal brews, allowing you to discover new flavors and styles.

Brewery Tours: Many brewery tours include guided tours of the brewing facilities. Knowledgeable guides or brewery staff will lead you through the brewing process, explaining how beer is made, from the ingredients to the fermentation and packaging.

Local Breweries: Cleveland's brewery scene is dynamic, with each brewery offering its own unique beers and atmosphere. You'll have the chance to explore a variety of brewery settings, from cozy taprooms to spacious beer gardens.

Travel to Cleveland Ohio

Craft Beer Education: Expect to learn about the craft beer culture, the history of the breweries you visit, and the significance of different beer styles. Guides often share interesting stories and facts about the breweries.

Food Pairings: Some brewery tours offer food pairings to complement the beer tastings. You may enjoy snacks, appetizers, or even full meals that are carefully matched with the beer selections.

Brewery Souvenirs: Many breweries have on-site gift shops where you can purchase merchandise such as branded glassware, clothing, and, of course, beer to take home with you.

Transportation: Brewery tours typically provide transportation between the breweries, ensuring a safe and convenient way to enjoy the tastings without worrying about driving.

Group Atmosphere: Brewery tours often have a fun and social atmosphere, making them an excellent choice for groups of friends, family outings, or even team-building events for coworkers.

Customizable Tours: Some tour operators offer customizable brewery tours, allowing you to select specific breweries or themes that align with your beer preferences.

Reservations: It's a good idea to make reservations for brewery tours in advance, especially during peak times or on weekends.

Local Craft Beer Scene: Cleveland's craft beer scene is constantly evolving, so you may want to research the latest breweries and tour options available during your visit.

Whether you're a craft beer enthusiast or just looking to enjoy a day of tasting local brews, a brewery tour in Cleveland offers a memorable and flavorful experience. It's an opportunity to savor the city's craft beer culture, support local breweries, and discover new favorite beers.

101. Visit the Nature Center at Shaker Lakes.

Visiting the Nature Center at Shaker Lakes in Cleveland is a wonderful way to connect with nature, explore wildlife, and learn about environmental conservation. Here's what you can expect when you visit this serene and educational nature center:

Location: The Nature Center at Shaker Lakes is located in the Shaker Heights neighborhood of Cleveland, providing easy access to nature within the city. Check the nature center's official website or local listings for the specific address and directions.

Natural Setting: The nature center is situated within a beautiful and peaceful natural setting, featuring several interconnected lakes, wetlands, forests, and meadows. It offers a serene escape from the urban environment and a chance to observe local wildlife.

Trails and Hiking: The center typically has well-maintained hiking trails that wind through the natural areas, providing opportunities for nature walks, birdwatching, and wildlife observation. Be sure to wear comfortable footwear and consider bringing binoculars for birdwatching.

Visitor Center: The visitor center is the heart of the Nature Center at Shaker Lakes. Inside, you'll find informative displays, exhibits, and educational materials related to the local ecosystem, wildlife, and environmental conservation efforts.

Educational Programs: The center often hosts a variety of educational programs, workshops, and events for visitors of all ages. These programs may cover topics such as ecology, wildlife, sustainable gardening, and more. Check the center's calendar for upcoming events.

Wildlife Observation: The nature center is a haven for wildlife, and you may encounter various species of birds, mammals, amphibians, and insects during your visit. Birdwatchers, in particular, will find the area rich in avian diversity.

Environmental Initiatives: The Nature Center at Shaker Lakes is typically involved in conservation and sustainability efforts. Learn about the center's initiatives aimed at protecting and preserving local ecosystems.

Picnicking: Some nature centers offer picnic areas or spots where you can enjoy a meal or snack amidst the natural surroundings. Consider bringing a picnic to make the most of your visit.

Travel to Cleveland Ohio

Photography: The picturesque landscapes and wildlife provide excellent opportunities for photography. Capture the beauty of nature and its inhabitants during your visit.

Accessibility: The nature center often strives to provide accessibility for all visitors, including those with disabilities. Inquire about specific accommodations you may need.

Visitor Information: Check the nature center's official website or contact them directly for information on hours of operation, special events, admission fees (if applicable), and any seasonal considerations.

A visit to the Nature Center at Shaker Lakes offers a tranquil escape into nature and a chance to appreciate the biodiversity of the region. It's an ideal destination for nature enthusiasts, families, educators, and anyone seeking a peaceful and educational experience in the heart of Cleveland's green spaces.

102.Attend the Cleveland Dragon Boat Festival.

Attending the Cleveland Dragon Boat Festival is a vibrant and cultural experience that celebrates the tradition of dragon boat racing, Chinese culture, and community spirit. Here's what you can expect when you participate in or attend this exciting festival:

Location: The Cleveland Dragon Boat Festival is typically held at a scenic waterfront location, often at Rivergate Park along the Cuyahoga River. Check the festival's official website or local event listings for the specific location and details.

Dragon Boat Racing: The highlight of the festival is the dragon boat races. Teams of paddlers, often comprised of community groups, corporations, or local organizations, compete in colorful dragon boats, which are long, narrow vessels decorated like dragons. Witness the thrilling races as teams paddle in unison to the beat of a drum.

Cultural Performances: In addition to the races, the festival often features a variety of cultural performances, including traditional Chinese dance, music, and martial arts demonstrations. These performances provide insight into Chinese culture and add to the festival's festive atmosphere.

Food and Beverages: You can savor a wide array of Asian cuisine and beverages from local vendors. Sample dishes like dim sum, dumplings, spring rolls, and bubble tea, among others. It's an opportunity to explore different flavors and culinary traditions.

Arts and Crafts: Browse through artisan stalls and craft booths showcasing Asian-inspired artwork, crafts, clothing, and souvenirs. You can find unique and handmade items while supporting local artisans.

Interactive Activities: Some festivals include interactive activities for attendees, such as calligraphy workshops, traditional tea ceremonies, or cultural games. These activities offer hands-on cultural experiences.

Dragon Boat Viewing: In addition to watching the races, you can often explore the dragon boats up close, learn about their construction, and even take guided tours of these magnificent vessels.

Children's Activities: The Cleveland Dragon Boat Festival is typically family-friendly, with activities and entertainment suitable for all ages. Children can enjoy face painting, crafts, and more.

Photography: The vibrant dragon boat races, colorful costumes, and cultural performances provide excellent opportunities for photography. Capture the energy and excitement of the festival.

Accessibility: Festival organizers typically aim to provide accessibility for all attendees, including those with disabilities. Inquire about specific accommodations you may need.

Tickets: Check the festival's official website or local event listings for information on admission fees (if applicable), ticket prices for dragon boat teams, and any special promotions. Some events may be ticketed, while others are free to attend.

Event Dates: The Cleveland Dragon Boat Festival is often held during specific dates or seasons, so be sure to check the festival's schedule and plan your visit accordingly.

Attending the Cleveland Dragon Boat Festival is an exhilarating way to immerse yourself in the excitement of dragon boat racing, learn about Chinese culture, and enjoy delicious Asian cuisine. Whether you're a sports enthusiast, a culture lover, or simply seeking a lively and community-centered event, this festival offers a memorable and spirited experience.

103. Explore the Rockefeller Park Greenhouse.

Exploring the Rockefeller Park Greenhouse in Cleveland offers a serene and immersive experience in a lush botanical setting. Here's what you can expect when you visit this delightful greenhouse:

Location: The Rockefeller Park Greenhouse is typically located in Rockefeller Park, within the University Circle neighborhood of Cleveland. Check the greenhouse's official website or local listings for the specific address and directions.

Botanical Collection: The greenhouse is home to a diverse and impressive collection of plants from around the world. You can explore a wide variety of exotic and tropical plants, including orchids, cacti, succulents, ferns, and many other species.

Greenhouse Rooms: The greenhouse complex is divided into different rooms or sections, each with its own unique theme and plant species. These rooms are typically organized to create specific environments that mimic the natural habitats of the plants on display.

Educational Exhibits: The Rockefeller Park Greenhouse often features educational exhibits and informational displays that provide insights into plant biology, conservation, and horticultural practices. You can learn about the importance of plants and their role in the environment.

Seasonal Displays: Depending on the time of your visit, you may encounter seasonal displays that celebrate holidays, special occasions, or particular plant species in bloom. These displays add a festive and ever-changing element to the greenhouse.

Tranquil Atmosphere: The greenhouse provides a tranquil and calming atmosphere, making it an ideal place for relaxation and contemplation. It's a peaceful oasis within the city where you can escape the hustle and bustle.

Photography: The lush greenery and colorful blooms offer excellent opportunities for photography. Bring your camera or smartphone to capture the beauty of the plants and the greenhouse's serene ambiance.

Accessibility: The Rockefeller Park Greenhouse typically aims to provide accessibility for all visitors, including those with disabilities. Inquire about specific accommodations you may need.

Visitor Information: Check the greenhouse's official website or contact them directly for information on hours of operation, admission fees (if applicable), and any seasonal considerations.

Gift Shop: Some greenhouses have on-site gift shops where you can purchase botanical-themed souvenirs, gardening supplies, and plant-related items.

Botanical Gardens: While visiting the Rockefeller Park Greenhouse, you may also want to explore the surrounding gardens and park areas in Rockefeller Park. These outdoor spaces offer additional opportunities to enjoy nature and beautiful landscapes.

A visit to the Rockefeller Park Greenhouse provides a refreshing and educational escape into the world of plants and horticulture. Whether you're a botany enthusiast, a nature lover, or simply seeking a tranquil environment, this greenhouse offers a delightful and rejuvenating experience in the heart of Cleveland.

104. Take a scenic drive along the Ohio & Erie Canal Towpath Trail.

Taking a scenic drive along the Ohio & Erie Canal Towpath Trail offers a picturesque journey through history and nature in the Cleveland area. Here's what you can expect when you embark on this scenic drive:

Location: The Ohio & Erie Canal Towpath Trail runs through several counties in Ohio, including the Cleveland area. Depending on your starting point and desired route, you can access different sections of the trail. The Cleveland area typically includes portions of the trail that pass through Cuyahoga County.

Travel to Cleveland Ohio

Historical Significance: The Ohio & Erie Canal Towpath Trail follows the path of the historic Ohio & Erie Canal, which played a pivotal role in the region's development during the 19th century. As you drive along the trail, you'll encounter remnants of the canal system, such as locks, bridges, and historic structures.

Scenic Beauty: The drive offers picturesque views of the Cuyahoga River, lush forests, wetlands, and scenic landscapes. Depending on the season, you can witness vibrant fall foliage, blooming wildflowers, and abundant wildlife.

Recreational Opportunities: The Ohio & Erie Canal Towpath Trail is a popular destination for outdoor enthusiasts. Along the drive, you may encounter hikers, cyclists, joggers, and birdwatchers enjoying the trail's recreational opportunities.

Trailheads: The trail typically features various trailheads and access points where you can park your vehicle and explore different sections of the towpath on foot or by bicycle. Some trailheads offer visitor centers with information and maps.

Historic Sites: Be on the lookout for historic sites and landmarks, including canal locks, interpretive signs, and museums that provide insight into the canal's history and significance.

Visitor Centers: Depending on the section of the trail you explore, you may come across visitor centers or interpretive facilities that offer exhibits, educational programs, and resources about the canal's history and the surrounding natural environment.

Seasonal Considerations: Keep in mind that the trail's scenery and accessibility can vary with the seasons. Spring and fall are often considered ideal times for a scenic drive, as the weather is pleasant and the landscapes are particularly beautiful.

Accessibility: The Ohio & Erie Canal Towpath Trail typically aims to provide accessibility for all visitors, including those with disabilities. Inquire about specific accommodations you may need at visitor centers or trailheads.

Visitor Information: Check the official website of the Ohio & Erie Canalway Coalition or contact them for detailed information about trail access points, maps, and any seasonal events or activities.

Driving along the Ohio & Erie Canal Towpath Trail offers a unique opportunity to connect with history, appreciate natural beauty, and explore the region's heritage. Whether you're interested in a leisurely drive, a scenic photography excursion, or a deeper exploration of the trail's offerings, this route provides a captivating and educational journey in the Cleveland area.

105. Visit the Cleveland Pops Orchestra.

Visiting the Cleveland Pops Orchestra offers a chance to enjoy live orchestral music performances in a vibrant and cultural setting. Here's what you can expect when you attend a concert by the Cleveland Pops Orchestra:

Location: The Cleveland Pops Orchestra typically performs in various venues across the Cleveland area, including concert halls, theaters, and cultural centers. Check the orchestra's official website or local event listings for specific concert locations and schedules.

Orchestral Performances: The Cleveland Pops Orchestra is known for its captivating orchestral performances. Attendees can expect to hear a wide range of musical compositions, including classical masterpieces, Broadway tunes, popular songs, and patriotic selections.

Conductor and Musicians: The orchestra is led by a skilled conductor, and its musicians are talented and accomplished instrumentalists. The ensemble's musicians often include members of the Cleveland Orchestra and other accomplished professionals.

Concert Themes: The Cleveland Pops Orchestra often presents concerts with specific themes or genres, catering to a diverse range of musical tastes. Concert themes may include pops classics, movie scores, holiday music, and more.

Guest Artists: Some concerts feature guest artists, such as renowned soloists, vocalists, or instrumentalists, who collaborate with the orchestra to create memorable performances.

Seasonal Concerts: The orchestra typically offers a seasonal concert schedule, which may include special performances for holidays like Christmas, New Year's, Independence Day, and more. These concerts often feature thematic music and festive elements.

Travel to Cleveland Ohio

Audience Engagement: During performances, the orchestra and conductor may engage with the audience, providing insights into the music, composers, and historical context. It's an opportunity to deepen your appreciation for the music.

Ticket Information: Check the orchestra's official website or contact them directly for information on ticket prices, availability, and any special promotions. Consider purchasing tickets in advance, especially for popular concerts.

Educational Outreach: The Cleveland Pops Orchestra may also be involved in educational outreach programs, offering opportunities for students and young musicians to engage with classical music.

Accessibility: Concert venues typically aim to provide accessibility for all attendees, including those with disabilities. Inquire about specific accommodations you may need.

Attire: While there is no strict dress code, many attendees choose to dress semi-formally or formally for orchestral performances. However, casual attire is also welcomed.

Concert Calendar: Check the orchestra's official website for a concert calendar, which provides information on upcoming performances, venues, and program details.

Attending a Cleveland Pops Orchestra concert is an enriching and cultural experience that allows you to immerse yourself in the world of classical and pops music. Whether you're a seasoned classical music enthusiast or new to orchestral performances, the orchestra's concerts offer a memorable and enjoyable evening of live music in the Cleveland area.

106.Attend a performance at the Near West Theatre.

Attending a performance at the Near West Theatre in Cleveland is a unique and immersive cultural experience that combines the arts with community involvement. Here's what you can expect when you attend a production at this theater:

People Who Know Publishing

Location: The Near West Theatre is typically located in the Gordon Square Arts District, a vibrant and artistic neighborhood in Cleveland. Check the theater's official website or local event listings for the specific address and directions.

Community Theater: Near West Theatre is a community-based theater, known for involving individuals of all ages and backgrounds, including volunteers and local performers. It focuses on providing opportunities for community members to participate in theatrical productions.

Diverse Productions: The theater presents a diverse range of theatrical productions, including musicals, plays, and original works. Productions often feature themes of social justice, inclusion, and community building.

Inclusive Casting: Near West Theatre is committed to inclusive casting, meaning that roles are open to individuals of all abilities and backgrounds. This approach creates a welcoming and diverse ensemble of performers.

Amateur and Professional: While the theater welcomes amateur actors and volunteers, it also collaborates with professional artists and directors to bring high-quality productions to the stage.

Engaging Performances: Productions at Near West Theatre are known for their engaging and energetic performances. The combination of local talent and professional guidance results in entertaining and thought-provoking shows.

Intimate Venue: The theater typically offers an intimate and cozy venue where the audience can feel close to the action on stage. This creates an immersive and personal theater experience.

Youth and Education: Near West Theatre often includes youth and educational programs, providing opportunities for young performers to participate in productions and develop their theatrical skills.

Audience Engagement: The theater may offer pre-show discussions, talkbacks with the cast and crew, and other opportunities for audience members to interact with the production and gain insights into the creative process.

Ticket Information: Check the theater's official website or contact them directly for information on ticket prices, show schedules, and any special promotions. Tickets for productions are typically available for purchase in advance.

Travel to Cleveland Ohio

Accessibility: The theater typically aims to provide accessibility for all attendees, including those with disabilities. Inquire about specific accommodations you may need.

Attire: Dress code at Near West Theatre is typically casual, although you may choose to dress up a bit if you prefer.

Parking: Depending on the location, the theater may offer on-site or nearby parking options. Check the theater's website for parking information.

Seasonal Productions: Near West Theatre often offers seasonal productions, so be sure to check the theater's schedule for information on upcoming shows and performance dates.

Attending a performance at Near West Theatre is not only an opportunity to enjoy live theater but also to engage with a welcoming and diverse community of artists and audience members. Whether you're a theater enthusiast or simply looking for an inclusive and culturally enriching experience, Near West Theatre offers a memorable and heartwarming theatrical journey in Cleveland.

107. Explore the Cultural Gardens at Wade Oval.

Exploring the Cultural Gardens at Wade Oval in Cleveland is a journey through a diverse and beautifully landscaped collection of gardens that celebrate various ethnic and cultural communities. Here's what you can expect when you visit these unique gardens:

Location: The Cultural Gardens at Wade Oval are typically situated in the University Circle neighborhood of Cleveland. Check the gardens' official website or local listings for the specific address and directions.

Cultural Diversity: The gardens are a remarkable tribute to Cleveland's cultural diversity and heritage. Each garden is dedicated to a specific ethnic or cultural group, and they collectively represent over 30 different communities. You'll have the opportunity to explore gardens representing countries and regions from around the world.

Garden Styles: Each cultural garden is designed in a style that reflects the culture it represents. This includes architectural elements, sculptures, and landscaping that pay homage to the traditions and aesthetics of the respective culture.

Peace and Unity: The Cultural Gardens at Wade Oval are a symbol of peace and unity among cultures. They serve as a reminder of the importance of understanding and appreciating cultural differences while celebrating shared values and aspirations.

Walking Path: The gardens are interconnected by a walking path that allows you to stroll through this cultural tapestry at your own pace. Walking through the gardens offers a serene and reflective experience.

Picnicking: Some visitors choose to bring picnic baskets and enjoy meals in the peaceful surroundings of the gardens. There are often designated areas where you can relax and savor your food.

Events and Festivals: Throughout the year, the Cultural Gardens host various events and festivals that celebrate different cultures through music, dance, food, and cultural presentations. Check the gardens' event calendar for upcoming celebrations.

Photography: The beautiful landscaping, sculptures, and architectural elements provide excellent opportunities for photography. Capture the vibrant colors, intricate details, and cultural symbolism of the gardens.

Educational Signage: Many gardens have educational signage that provides information about the cultural significance of the garden, the history of the community it represents, and key facts about the culture.

Accessibility: The Cultural Gardens typically aim to provide accessibility for all visitors, including those with disabilities. Inquire about specific accommodations you may need.

Visitor Information: Check the gardens' official website or contact them directly for information on hours of operation, admission (if applicable), guided tours, and any seasonal considerations.

Visiting the Cultural Gardens at Wade Oval is an enriching and contemplative experience that allows you to explore the world's cultural diversity in one serene and harmonious setting. Whether you're interested in cultural heritage, landscape design, or simply seeking a peaceful escape, the Cultural Gardens offer a memorable and educational journey in the heart of Cleveland.

108. Go paddleboarding on the Cuyahoga River.

Paddleboarding on the Cuyahoga River in Cleveland is a fantastic way to enjoy outdoor recreation and experience the city from a unique perspective. Here's what you can expect when you go paddleboarding on the Cuyahoga River:

Location: The Cuyahoga River flows through the heart of Cleveland, providing multiple access points and areas where you can launch your paddleboard. Some popular locations for paddleboarding on the Cuyahoga River include Merwin's Wharf, Rivergate Park, and the Flats East Bank.

Scenic Views: Paddleboarding on the Cuyahoga River offers scenic views of the city skyline, waterfront neighborhoods, and natural landscapes. You'll have the opportunity to take in the beauty of Cleveland from the water.

Paddleboard Rentals: If you don't have your own paddleboard, there are often rental facilities and outfitters located near the river where you can rent paddleboards, paddles, and safety equipment.

Skill Levels: Paddleboarding on the Cuyahoga River is suitable for all skill levels, from beginners to experienced paddlers. The river's calm sections are ideal for novices, while more experienced paddlers may explore its entire length.

Safety: Safety is a top priority when paddleboarding. Make sure to wear a personal flotation device (PFD) and have basic paddleboarding skills, such as maintaining balance and maneuvering the board.

Guided Tours: Some outfitters and paddleboard rental facilities offer guided tours on the Cuyahoga River. These tours may provide insights into the river's history, ecology, and landmarks.

Wildlife: Keep an eye out for wildlife along the riverbanks and in the water. You may spot birds, fish, and other aquatic creatures while paddleboarding.

Waterfront Dining: After your paddleboarding adventure, you can often find waterfront restaurants and bars in the area where you can enjoy a meal or refreshments while taking in the river views.

Group Activities: Paddleboarding on the Cuyahoga River can be a fun group activity. Consider organizing a paddleboarding outing with friends or family for a memorable experience.

Seasonal Considerations: The availability of paddleboarding on the Cuyahoga River may be weather-dependent, so it's a good idea to check with rental facilities or outfitters for seasonal hours and conditions.

Accessibility: Some paddleboarding rental facilities aim to provide accessibility for all visitors, including those with disabilities. Inquire about specific accommodations you may need.

Attire: Wear comfortable and weather-appropriate clothing, as well as sunscreen and a hat to protect yourself from the sun. You may also want to bring a waterproof bag for personal items.

Reservations: If you plan to rent paddleboarding equipment or join a guided tour, it's a good idea to make reservations in advance, especially during peak seasons.

Paddleboarding on the Cuyahoga River offers a memorable way to explore Cleveland's waterways and enjoy the city's scenic beauty. Whether you're looking for a peaceful solo excursion or a group adventure, paddleboarding provides a refreshing and active experience in the heart of the city.

109. Attend the Feast of St. Augustine in Tremont.

Attending the Feast of St. Augustine in Tremont is a vibrant and cultural celebration that brings together the community to honor the patron saint and enjoy food, music, and festivities. Here's what you can expect when you attend this annual event:

Location: The Feast of St. Augustine typically takes place in the Tremont neighborhood of Cleveland. Specific locations and event details may vary from

Travel to Cleveland Ohio

year to year, so it's advisable to check the event's official website or local listings for the most up-to-date information on the festival's location.

Religious Celebration: The Feast of St. Augustine is a religious celebration that commemorates St. Augustine of Hippo, a revered Christian theologian and philosopher. The festival often begins with a religious procession or Mass to honor the saint.

Cultural Festival: In addition to its religious significance, the Feast of St. Augustine also features a cultural festival with a lively atmosphere. You can expect to find a variety of activities and attractions that celebrate the community's heritage.

Food and Cuisine: Food is a central aspect of the festival, and you can sample a wide range of delicious dishes, including traditional Italian and Mediterranean cuisine. Look for food stalls and vendors offering specialties such as pasta, pizza, cannoli, and more.

Music and Entertainment: Live music and entertainment are key components of the Feast of St. Augustine. You can enjoy performances by local bands, dance groups, and musicians, adding to the festive atmosphere.

Carnival Games and Rides: The festival often includes carnival games and rides that are fun for both children and adults. It's a great place for families to enjoy rides, games, and entertainment.

Art and Crafts: Browse through artisan booths and craft vendors offering handmade goods, artwork, jewelry, and other unique items. It's an opportunity to shop for souvenirs and support local artisans.

Procession: Some festivals feature a procession through the streets of Tremont, where participants carry religious icons and statues of St. Augustine. This procession is often a highlight of the event.

Community Involvement: The Feast of St. Augustine is a community-oriented event that encourages participation from residents and visitors alike. It's a chance to connect with the local community and learn about its traditions.

Accessibility: Event organizers typically aim to provide accessibility for all attendees, including those with disabilities. Inquire about specific accommodations you may need.

Attire: While there is no strict dress code, many attendees choose to wear festive or cultural attire to celebrate the occasion.

Event Dates: The Feast of St. Augustine is an annual event, so check the festival's official website or local event listings for information on dates and schedules.

Admission: Admission to the festival may be free or have a nominal fee. Check the event's official website for details on admission and any ticketed activities.

The Feast of St. Augustine in Tremont offers a lively blend of religious tradition, cultural celebration, and community spirit. Whether you're interested in experiencing the cultural heritage of the neighborhood, savoring delicious cuisine, or simply enjoying the festive atmosphere, this annual event provides an engaging and memorable experience in Cleveland.

110. Visit the Cleveland Pickle.

Visiting the Cleveland Pickle is a tasty adventure that allows you to savor a variety of gourmet pickles and deli-style sandwiches. Here's what you can expect when you visit this popular pickle shop:

Location: The Cleveland Pickle is typically located in downtown Cleveland. Check the shop's official website or local listings for the specific address and hours of operation.

Pickle Selection: As the name suggests, the Cleveland Pickle is known for its wide selection of pickles. You can explore an array of pickled vegetables, ranging from classic dill pickles to unique and creative flavor combinations. Try different pickle varieties to find your favorite.

Deli-Style Sandwiches: In addition to pickles, the Cleveland Pickle offers a menu of deli-style sandwiches that feature their house-cured meats and pickles. These sandwiches are often made to order and can include options like corned beef, pastrami, turkey, and more.

Creative Flavors: The shop is known for its creative approach to pickling. You may find pickles with unusual flavor profiles, such as spicy sriracha, sweet and tangy bread and butter, or even specialty pickles like pickled grapes or pickled green tomatoes.

Travel to Cleveland Ohio

Local Ingredients: The Cleveland Pickle often sources local and high-quality ingredients for its pickles and sandwiches, contributing to the fresh and flavorful offerings.

Catering: If you have a special event or gathering, the Cleveland Pickle may offer catering services that include pickle platters, sandwich trays, and other options.

Retail Products: Some pickle shops offer retail products, allowing you to purchase jars of your favorite pickles to enjoy at home. Check if the Cleveland Pickle offers this option.

Friendly Atmosphere: The shop typically aims to provide a friendly and welcoming atmosphere for visitors. It's a great place to grab a quick and satisfying meal or snack.

Menu Variety: While pickles and sandwiches are the primary offerings, the Cleveland Pickle may also have sides, soups, and other items on its menu. Be sure to explore the full range of options.

Attire: Dress code at the Cleveland Pickle is typically casual. Come as you are to enjoy a delicious meal.

Operating Hours: Check the shop's official website or contact them directly for information on their operating hours, as they may vary.

Whether you're a pickle enthusiast or simply looking for a flavorful and satisfying meal, a visit to the Cleveland Pickle offers a unique culinary experience. Sample a variety of pickles, indulge in deli-style sandwiches, and savor the creative flavors that make this pickle shop a popular destination in Cleveland.

Conclusion

Cleveland, Ohio, is a story of resilience, growth, and transformation. From its humble beginnings as a small settlement along the Cuyahoga River in the early 19th century, Cleveland evolved into a thriving industrial and cultural hub by the 20th century. It played a pivotal role in the industrialization of the United States, particularly in the steel and manufacturing sectors.

The city's economic fortunes rose and fell with the times, experiencing both periods of prosperity and challenges. The Great Depression and deindustrialization of the late 20th century brought hardships, but Cleveland's determination to adapt and diversify its economy led to the emergence of new industries, including healthcare, finance, and technology.

Cleveland's rich cultural heritage is exemplified by its world-class cultural institutions, such as the Cleveland Museum of Art and the Rock and Roll Hall of Fame, which celebrate art, music, and innovation. The city's sports teams, including the Cleveland Indians, Cleveland Cavaliers, and Cleveland Browns, have also contributed to its identity and sense of community.

Today, Cleveland is a vibrant and dynamic city that continues to reinvent itself. It boasts a diverse population, a thriving arts scene, revitalized neighborhoods, and a commitment to sustainability and environmental stewardship. The city's waterfront redevelopment, including the Flats East Bank and the Lake Erie shoreline, has brought new life to its downtown area.

Cleveland's history serves as a testament to the spirit of its residents who have persevered through challenges and embraced change. It is a city that honors its industrial past while looking toward a future driven by innovation, culture, and a sense of community. As it continues to evolve, Cleveland remains a city with a rich history and a promising future.

Travel to Cleveland Ohio

If you enjoyed, please leave a 5-star Amazon Review

To get a free list of people who knows publishing top places to travel all around the world, click this link
https://bit.ly/peoplewhoknowtravel

References

Rcsprinter123, CC BY-SA 3.0 <https://creativecommons.org/licenses/by-sa/3.0>, via Wikimedia Commons

https://pixabay.com/photos/platter-food-starters-meal-feast-2009590/

Printed in Great Britain
by Amazon